Praise for *Five Steps to Rapid Employment*

"*Five Steps to Rapid Employment* is proof that Jay Block is not only a fine author and first rate coach, but a man of principle, integrity, and compassion."

— DICK BOLLES, *author of* What Color Is Your Parachute?

"A true A-to-Z approach to landing the job of your choice regardless of market conditions. Jay's book empowers job seekers to take control of their future by being proactive, resourceful, and innovative— including building a referral network both online and off. If you are serious about landing a quality job quickly in today's job market, this book will practically guarantee your success."

— BOB BURG, *author of* Endless Referrals *and* The Go-Giver

"Jay Block is an industry icon and has taken his place as one of the career-coaching industry's most innovative thinkers and contributors. He is always challenging traditional ways of thinking to develop new techniques and tools to inspire people to achieve career and life success. *Five Steps to Rapid Employment* is his most important work to date. Jay continues to find new and effective approaches to challenge us all to successfully navigate through today's complex and ever-changing job market to secure meaningful employment."

— FRANK X. FOX, *Executive Director, Professional Association of Résumé Writers and Career Coaches*

"Jay has written a one-of-a-kind book combining motivational techniques with job search innovation. Jay offers fresh, exciting, and timely strategies, tools, and processes to help people land jobs in competitive job markets. This book is way overdue, is enjoyable and easy to read, and offers encouragement and specifics to successfully meet the challenges and complexities of today's job market. This is mandatory reading for anyone seeking a new/better job."

— SUSAN LEVENTHAL, *Manager, Professional Placement Network, Workforce One, South Florida*

"This book is a must-read for all job seekers in today's competitive job market. Whether you're a graduating student or a transitional worker, you will benefit from all the simple motivational techniques and career management tips that are offered from cover to cover. This book should be required reading for all graduates before entering the job market."

—SHERRY ZYLKA, PhD, *Provost, Wayne County Community College District, MI*

5 STEPS to RAPID EMPLOYMENT

Other Titles from Jay Block

5 STEPS to RAPID EMPLOYMENT

The Job You Want at the Pay You Deserve

JAY A. BLOCK

Updated edition of
101 Best Ways to Land a Job in Troubled Times

McGraw Hill Education

New York   Chicago   San Francisco   Athens   London   Madrid
Mexico City   Milan   New Delhi   Singapore   Sydney   Toronto

1 2 3 4 5 6 7 8 9 0   QFR/QFR   1 2 0 9 8 7 6 5 4

ISBN 978-0-07-183930-3
MHID 0-07-183930-5

e-ISBN 978-0-07-183931-0
e-MHID 0-07-183931-3

Library of Congress Cataloging-in-Publication Data
Block, Jay A.
  5 steps to rapid employment : the job you want at the pay you deserve / by Jay A. Block.
      pages cm
  Includes index.
  ISBN 978-0-07-183930-3 (alk. paper)—ISBN 0-07-183930-5 (alk. paper)
1. Job hunting. I. Title.
  HF5382.7.B5947 2014
  650.14—dc23

                                                    2014008783

McGraw-Hill Education books are available at special quantity discounts to use as premiums and sales promotions or for use in corporate training programs. To contact a representative, please visit the Contact Us pages at www.mhprofessional.com.

To my son, Ryco . . . the brightest star in my universe

CONTENTS

STEP 5 Taking Action   185
Master a Few Self-Marketing Skills...
Then Take Massive Action to Land a Job Quickly

SUSAN D. COREY,
M.ED., CWDP, BES, MS

Southeast Michigan Community Alliance;
Manager of Workforce Development

Board Member, The National Association of
Workforce Development Professionals

Dear Reader:

Every once in a while you meet someone using his gifts and talents to really make a difference in people's lives. Jay Block is that person. His message is a clarion call for you to take action in your life: to provide a guide on how to survive and thrive in the new global job market and to motivate yourself to achieve all that you are capable of and deserve. Finally, someone provides an upbeat and inspirational approach to career management and job change! Jay combines commanding motivational techniques with a highly effective five-step strategic process for conducting a successful job campaign. He makes the process of pursuing and landing a new job inspirational and enjoyable. He shows you how to remain fearless, hopeful, confident, and highly engaged in the wake of adversity and setbacks. And the good news is that the process of landing a job is simple. This book will show you just how simple. The only thing you need to do is work diligently at what is simple.

Five Steps to Rapid Employment will be the only resource you will need to land a new job or discover your true calling. Today's competitive, global job market requires new ways of thinking, new beliefs, effective and inspiring processes, and a renewed sense of hope. Jay is a pioneer in the career management industry, by definition, an innovative thinker. The foundation of his success—which he measures by the success of his clients—was established over the past 20 years by constantly applying new ways of thinking so you can better plan your career and achieve your goals. Actually, this book is not only a book on job transition and career management; it is also a book on how to significantly improve your quality of life. You will be inspired to take specific actions that will lead to a "richer" life!

So if you are ready to enrich your quality of life and take control of your career, immerse yourself in the material Jay presents in this book. Cherish the time you spend working through the processes Jay introduces. Revel in the experience of approaching the entire job campaign process with a whole new attitude and a whole new set of tools and strategies. And then watch your new future unfold!

PREFACE

I was fired by one of my best friends in 1992. More on this later. But first I want you to know that this book was written for you, and I want you to think of me as your personal coach, one who truly cares about you and your future... because I do! I have worked with thousands of people from around the world to help them identify, pursue, and secure well-paying jobs and rewarding opportunities—quickly! Though you and I, most likely, have not met formally, I fully understand and empathize with what you may be currently experiencing and the emotional roller coaster you might be riding at this time in your life.

This book is different from most other job search books because I reject the idea that job search is an effective activity, or that it works at all. How many job seekers have difficulty falling asleep at night because they are so excited about the prospects of conducting their job search the following morning? Answer: Approximately zero!

As you will see during our time together, landing a new job or workplace opportunity is a process, not a search. Whether you are a graduating student or a seasoned professional, landing your next job can be compared with planning and orchestrating a political campaign. Politicians who seek to get "hired" for elected office do not conduct a political search; they conduct a strategic campaign. And so must you. And once you embrace this new way of thinking, you will (1) have much more control over your future, (2) secure rewarding opportunities quickly at the pay you deserve, and (3) genuinely enjoy the process, as unlikely as this may seem. But you see, successful campaigners revel in the campaign process, knowing that a positive approach always provides the best chance to achieve positive results!

I have worked with people who have been unexpectedly terminated, downsized, rightsized, and capsized from their jobs. I have worked with those who have bosses from you-know-where, who are stressed out from working in toxic environments, and who are toiling every day at jobs that are downright uninspiring. I have worked with college grads who were scared to death of making the transition from the comfort of the campus to the *real world*. Many clients and audiences that I have addressed over the past two decades are still in "What do I want to be when I grow up?" mode. And yet others are hampered by golden handcuffs, tethered to an unexciting and taxing job. They are unable to seek out new opportunities because economic and financial considerations are such that they can't relinquish their current jobs and because they are so exhausted and stressed out at the end of the day, they haven't the energy to pursue better opportunities. Finally, I have worked with employees wanting to start their own enterprises as well as entrepreneurs wanting to convert to employees.

So I feel like I know you personally as well as the challenges you face. When I graduated from the University of New Hampshire in the mid-1970s, in the midst of a severe recession, the unemployment rate was near 8 percent. It took me months to find a management trainee job that paid just 10 cents over minimum wage! However, I accepted the job and worked my way up to an operations manager in just six months. Then, at age 26, I quit my job and started my own company and sold it for a handsome profit at age 30. I subsequently went into business in partnership with a French company and proceeded to lose just about everything by the time I was 31. I came close to bankruptcy. I continued to struggle to find my place in the labor market over the next seven years. Then, in 1991, one of my best friends hired me as his marketing director. A year later he fired me. Humiliation can't begin to describe the emotional anguish I felt. So there I was, 39 years old, broke and broken. I had lost my confidence, my dignity, and any hope for a better future. I was forced to reinvent myself but had no idea how to do it. So I sought out and worked with some of the world's most reputable coaches, pored through hundreds and hundreds of books and audiobooks, and, by the age of 45, found my passions, emerged as an industry leader, and became a well-respected author and international trainer. The point I am making is that I have experienced much of what you may be experiencing today. But I succeeded, as will you, if you simply follow the Five Steps to Rapid Employment process outlined in this book.

Since 1993, I have interviewed thousands of hiring managers, HR professionals, and executive recruiters to determine what they look for and what is important to them when they are hiring. Armed with this information, I discovered that most of what you've been taught about the job search makes no sense, is contrary to effective and accepted methods of marketing, and is an activity filled with fear and anxiety, not excitement and optimism. So I set out to identify a commonsense and motivational process that would successfully work for anyone... and found it! Since then, I have assisted tens of thousands of people to clearly identify, pursue, and achieve meaningful and well-paying jobs quickly. And it is this information I want to share with you in this book.

So I thank you for choosing this book and for spending time here with me. I invite you to soak up the ideas and strategies I will share with you so you too can achieve all that you deserve. And don't ever sell yourself short—you deserve so much! Treat our time together as an exciting and life-changing journey that will do for you what it did for me—give you confidence, self-respect, and genuine enthusiasm to create that future you so richly deserve.

5 STEPS
to RAPID
EMPLOYMENT

WHAT YOU NEED TO KNOW BEFORE WE START

How Beliefs Affect Outcome

Most successful endeavors are a result of successful processes. There is a process we go through to graduate high school and college. There is a process for baking a cake, for writing a book, for conducting a marriage ceremony, and for building and managing a business enterprise. And there is a process for quickly landing a well-paying, rewarding job. The challenge is that if you were to ask 25 employment experts what the process is, you'd get either a bunch of blank stares or 25 different, oftentimes conflicting, opinions. I would venture to guess that most would simply provide the same advice that has been circulating for about 75 years now; namely, put your résumé together and work on interviewing skills.

Good News: The Process Is Easy!

The good news is that the process for quickly landing the job you want at the pay you deserve is an easy five-step process. All you need to know is what the steps are and then work hard on each step. And this would be an appropriate time to dispel any idea that there is some magic pill that you can take to land that next best job. There isn't one. But the five-step process is easy; anyone can follow the steps successfully and confidently. You only have to work hard at what's easy. The reason why so many people struggle with their job search efforts is because they don't know the process or they don't follow it. They treat the activity as a search, not a well-planned and orchestrated campaign. The Five Steps to Rapid Employment is a proven, highly successful process that will work for anyone who commits to it.

Change Your Thinking; Change Your Life

You are about to embark on a job campaign—not a job search. Having said this, let me pose to you some questions to think about: Are you planning on conducting your campaign with high energy, enthusiasm, and confidence? What are your beliefs about seeking out a new job or identifying a new career? What are your beliefs about the economy and the current state of the job market? What are your beliefs about résumés and interviewing? What are your beliefs about how many hours a week you will invest in landing a new, more rewarding job? And what are your beliefs about how others will perceive you if you have been downsized or are unemployed?

You see, most of your beliefs are merely your thoughts that have been conditioned or programmed into your mind. For instance, when you experience a job loss, the automatic conditioned pattern of response is to think that this event is devastating, humiliating, and painful. You involuntarily associate fear with joblessness because that is how you've been conditioned to react. On the other hand, you can consciously and authentically change your beliefs about job loss and look at the event as a gift and as an opportunity to improve yourself, your income, and your future. The situation of losing a job is just that, a job loss. The emotions associated with this event, be they positive or negative, are derived from your beliefs—how you think— about losing a job. The same holds true for college graduates. Upon leaving academia and entering the job market, your beliefs affect your outcome. If you believe you will land a job rapidly, you probably will. If you believe it will be a long and painful experience, most likely it will be. In other words, it's not the events in your life that make the difference between happiness and unhappiness or between success and failure. Rather, it's the meaning and beliefs that you associate with those events. It's how you think.

Sarah Hightower Hill, president and CEO of Chandler-Hill Partners, a national executive outplacement firm, says:

> Who is doing your thinking? With the onslaught of 24-hour news and a challenging economy and job market being the primary topics of conversation by all of the talking heads and their analysts, it's difficult if not impossible to keep from being prejudiced in some way by what you hear. Recently I had a conversation with an executive client who was downsized. I was surprised when he told me that he thought it best to wait six to nine months before beginning his campaign because he felt there were few jobs available at the time in his particular industry. This client had a master's degree, plenty of experience, a professional designation and, truth be known, there were plenty of jobs available in his industry. Yet, because the national news, family members, and friends convinced him otherwise, he was willing to put off his job campaign for six to nine months. What would be the cost of that mistake? He had been earning $150k a year, so the cost of waiting six months would be a minimum of $75k. Always question who is doing your thinking because, many times, it's based on erroneous or misleading data and information.

In one of the first books ever published on career management, *Pick Your Job and Land It!*, published in 1938, authors Sidney Edlund and Mary Edlund made it clear that one's mental outlook (beliefs) determines outcome. In 1932, during the Great Depression, a good friend of the Edlunds lost his job and associated massive pain and a sense of despair with this event. The Edlunds helped their friend change the meaning of the event by helping him to change his beliefs. First, they pointed out that if he were to associate the idea of having fun with pursuing a new job, even with a 23.6 percent unemployment rate, he'd not only succeed in finding a new job quickly, but actually enjoy the process. The Edlunds also challenged their friend to change his beliefs about the job hunt itself. They suggested he look at it, not as a job hunt where he would be begging for jobs, but rather as a marketing and sales campaign where he offered valuable services that would benefit a company during difficult economic times.

In an economy where almost one in four people was out of work, this person was offered a job in less than a month because he changed his beliefs and his way of thinking. By changing his thinking, he changed his organizational strategies and methods of securing a new job. And to further drive home the fact that when you change your thinking, you can change any aspect of your life, the Edlunds noted that their friend actually beat out two close acquaintances and one family member of the hiring manager because he raised the bar of conducting an efficient high-impact campaign by communicating his value and his ability to make significant contributions at a time when it was needed the most.

You Control How You Think

Humans have the unique ability to change whenever they make the decision to do so. How you deal with adversity will shape your life more than almost anything else. If you associate pain, fear, and failure with losing a job or seeking a job, you may begin to believe that there's nothing you can do to make things better. You'll risk developing a sense of hopelessness or outright depression. These beliefs are destructive beliefs, and success achievement becomes almost impossible. On the other hand, when you realize that your belief system is not healthy emotionally and is not supporting your goals, ambitions, and potential, you can change how you think instantly! Nothing has to change in order for you to feel better about something except the meaning you give to it based on the thoughts you attach to it. *Simply stated, when you change your beliefs, you change your life!*

Is the Glass Half Empty or Half Full?

One of the best examples of the power of a belief is that age-old question, is the glass half empty or half full? If you perceive the glass as half empty, you'll probably have an empty and painful experience. If you alter your belief and view the glass as half full, you'll have a much better chance of experiencing a feeling of optimism, hope, and pleasure. Same glass, same amount of liquid in the glass, but different emotions and feelings based on your beliefs—how you think!

No human being had ever run a mile in under four minutes. However, in 1954 Roger Banister did just that. But there's a greater story hidden behind this story. After Banister did what no human had ever accomplished, just two months later, his record was broken by John Landy, followed by a host of runners that began running the mile in under four minutes. Can you begin to see how changing a belief can result in an almost miraculous achievement? Once Banister broke the four-minute-mile barrier, he also broke the belief barrier for others. As a result, runners instantly adopted a new belief that breaking the four-minute mile was achievable. Once you believe that you can land a job quickly after college or following a job loss or when it is time to seek a new job opportunity, because others have successfully done so, you get a renewed sense of confidence and a strong feeling of certainty that you, too, can achieve the same successful results.

The bottom line here is that you determine how you think at any given time based on how you manage and control your thoughts and beliefs. And this is important, because many traditional job search beliefs will be challenged throughout this book, and you must be open to examining and changing your beliefs about the entire process of career management and job transition.

What Are Your Beliefs About Landing a New Job?

Consider the following beliefs and the consequences, both positive and negative, that would result if you were to adopt one versus the other:

> This is a challenging economy, and there are no good jobs available.

> This is a challenging economy, but there are plenty of well-paying jobs just waiting for me if I work smarter, harder, and more strategically than my competitors.

> The job search is a painful and humiliating experience.

The job campaign is an enjoyable and character-building
endeavor.

It will take me forever to land a new job.
Armed with the right tools and strategies, I will land a new job
quickly.

I'll never find another job that will pay me what I was earning
before.
I know my value, the results I can produce, and the benefits I
bring to a new employer. This will allow me to land a better-
paying job in no time.

My family and friends will look down at me because I don't have
a job; this is embarrassing and humiliating.
With a confident attitude, my family and friends will support my
job campaign efforts and will be a positive influence in
landing my next job.

My résumé must conform to traditional standards and blend in
with all other résumés.
My résumé can be an exciting and informative marketing document that communicates my value and sets me apart from my
competition.

Résumés are only beneficial for getting my foot in the door.
Résumés are important documents that identify value, instill a
sense of self-confidence, and will strengthen me as an interviewee so I can quickly land a new, more rewarding job.

An interview is a forum where I am judged, and I don't like
being judged.
An interview is just an encounter where two parties gather
together to determine whether they can meet each other's
needs in an amicable and friendly manner.

I don't need a written plan of action to get a job. I'll just wake up
every day and wing it.

If I fail to develop a written strategic action plan, I can expect to fail; so I will develop the best written plan possible to achieve my job goals in the same way a general develops a written battle plan.

I hate networking. I'll never get a good job because I don't have a strong network of contacts.
I'll enjoy the process of establishing a *personal sales team*, made up of people I know and new relationships I will cultivate that will assist me to land a good job quickly.

I am too old to get a new job. There is definite age discrimination against older workers like me.
I will land a new job based on my ability to produce significant results. Age has nothing to do with getting a new job.

I can't afford to spend money on getting a new job because I have no job.
I can't afford *not* to invest in getting a new job even if I have no job, because if I don't invest in my future, I may not have one. Didn't I invest in college before I had a job offer?

Beliefs Will Either Empower or Limit Success Achievement

No doubt you are well aware of the concept of the self-fulfilling prophecy. The definition of a self-fulfilling prophecy is that negative beliefs predict or manifest negative behavior. Interestingly enough, we don't often associate the self-fulfilling prophecy with positive beliefs to manifest positive events. But in truth, your beliefs, whether they are positive or negative, empowering or limiting, will determine behavior and influence outcome. The concept of the self-fulfilling prophecy is normally associated with negative beliefs that result in limited achievement or failure. The challenge here is that this idea goes against the natural law of success. The fact of the matter is, if you associate positive beliefs with deep emotion, you can predict and manifest positive events. The self-fulfilling prophecy works both ways!

SUMMARY

Chekhov said that "man is what he believes," and that is certainly true when you begin the process of orchestrating a job campaign or dealing with work-related issues. I ask that you simply become aware of what your beliefs are and then ask yourself, "Do they empower me, or do they limit me in my quest for a better future, a better quality of life?" And if your belief system doesn't empower you to the extent you feel it could, know that you only need to adopt and embrace new beliefs that will fuel future success and promote achievement and personal happiness. One of the greatest gifts that human beings have is the ability to change their thinking, to change their beliefs, to change their lives.

Now it's time to embark on the five-step process that will catapult you from where you are to where you want to be. The five-step process includes:

1. *Learning how to ride the emotional roller coaster.* How to manage fear and negative emotions to secure rapid employment.
2. *Defining your goal.* Define workplace goals that inspire your life.
3. *Using value-based résumés and self-marketing tools.* Average résumés and online profiles won't attract the job you want at the pay you deserve.
4. *Creating a meticulous action plan.* A written strategic plan is your GPS to rapid employment.
5. *Taking action.* Master a few self-marketing skills... then take massive action to land a job quickly.

1

LEARNING HOW TO RIDE THE EMOTIONAL ROLLER COASTER

How to Manage Fear and Negative Emotions to Secure Rapid Employment

Arguably, two of the most painful occurrences in life are the loss of a loved one and the loss of a job. That being said and given your own situation, even if you haven't lost a job but are looking for one, what emotions are you feeling at this moment? Are you stunned, terrified, or filled with self-doubt? Are you experiencing high anxiety or even bouts of depression? Are you in a place called "I can't believe this is happening to me" or "How will I ever get through this?" These are just some of the emotions experienced by people whose lives are turned upside down when they lose their jobs, or who leave college to enter the workplace, or who, for whatever reason, find themselves seeking new opportunities in highly competitive job markets.

Regardless of what you are facing, in most cases, worry takes over and emotions go uncontrollably berserk. Initial questions will pervade your thoughts: "Will I survive this?" "Why did this happen to me?" "How long will I have to live at home?" "How long before I land a good job?" "Where will the money come from?" "Will I be able to keep my home?" "How will this affect my quality of life?" "Will I be a burden to my family?" The worst-case scenario takes center stage in the theater of your mind, and fear plays the starring role.

Landing a new job begins when you constructively and proactively manage and control your fears and negative emotions. Success is born from a fearless constitution. There are two primary components for effectively managing job loss, transitioning from education to the workplace, and securing a new job for any reason. The first is to assume personal responsibility and maintain a confident and positive attitude. The second is to use your peak-performing state of mind to plan and execute a flawless job campaign. You must become an educated, determined, and optimistic campaigner to effectively recover from job loss or land a new job in today's competitive job market. The information contained in Step 1 goes far beyond the idea of positive thinking. You will be introduced to specific techniques and strategies to empower you to remain positive and to manage your fears and emotions no matter what challenges or adversities you face. By doing so, you become an empowered, proactive participant in securing a new opportunity quickly and confidently.

First, a Few Words About Fear

Fear is normal—it can't be eliminated, nor should it be ignored. Fear must be conquered. It's been proved that landing a new, more rewarding job begins as soon as you learn how to conquer your fear and manage your mindset. In fact, if you don't acknowledge your fear, you'll become more at risk psychologically. Disarming and conquering your fear begins with recognizing its presence, accepting it, and taking action to manage it. And fear grips not just job seekers, but all those who are part of their circle of influence—spouses, children, parents, and friends.

This chapter contains authoritative information and strategies to motivate and empower everyone involved in the job campaign process to effectively deal with fear and its attendant crippling emotions such as guilt, resentment, doubt, helplessness, and feelings of being overwhelmed. In the wake of some of life's most difficult moments, courage and confidence become the conquering heroes. They help you become courageous in the wake of fear, negativity, pessimism, and stress in your efforts to rapidly land the job you want at the pay you deserve.

John Costello was a sales professional working in his family's business. He was unable to meet his financial obligations for himself and his son, Francesco, and he sought a new job.

> My emotions were on a constant roller-coaster ride. One day I was hopeful that my contacts would help me find a new position. Then anger, fear, and despair took over. I realized I was going to need help working through my emotions. And when I learned how to take control of my emotions, I immediately took control of my future in a positive and effective manner and landed the job I wanted in less than two months.

A positive attitude and confident approach to landing a new job not only will make the associated traumas and dramas bearable, but will also result in securing a new job quickly and gratifyingly. International job coach Martin Buckland, principal of Elite Executive Career Management Services headquartered in Ontario, Canada, says, "Controlling negative emotions in a positive way is critical to any job campaign. The more out of control you are emotionally, the longer the campaign will take, and chances are, you won't land the kind of job you really want. I work as hard with clients on their emotions as I do on their résumés."

So as you begin your journey to secure a new opportunity, you must embrace two critical components:

1. Adopt a healthy and positive outlook about how best to cope with and work through your fears, negative emotions, and life's unexpected bumps in the road.
2. Master the 10 principles of success and the four emotional channeling techniques introduced later in this chapter to help you maintain a positive, healthy state of mind.

Your Quality of Life Is the Quality of Your Emotions

Your quality of life—and that includes how you feel—is the quality of your emotions. It's not what you drive, where you live, or what you're experiencing that matters; it's how you feel about what you drive, where you live, or what you're experiencing that makes all the difference. Managing your emotions and attitudes is about not allowing anyone or anything to determine how you feel regardless of the challenges you face. You have the ultimate power to determine how you feel at any given time and in any situation.

There are so many variables that influence how you feel. The irony is that if you're like most people, you allow everything and everyone, except you, to determine your emotional state of mind. Said differently, you allow external influences to dictate your emotions. Advertisers, television programs, and the media are external influences. Parents, family members, and friends are external influences. Teachers, professors, and spiritual leaders are external influences. Even employment professionals—including job coaches, authors, HR managers, and executive recruiters—are external influences. Most of the time, you allow other people and other people's expectations and advice to dictate how you feel. But seldom do you allow yourself to determine how you feel based on your own conscious thoughts and expectations of yourself. Your reactions and emotions are a result of subconscious or conditioned beliefs rather than reason and common sense. In others words, you simply react in a fear-based, negative manner to situations, rather than rationally and constructively address and manage them. And the reason for this is simple—you've never been taught how to manage fear and negativity.

Destructive, negative, and fear-based mindsets create emotions that harm you and others. They are emotions that damage the job campaign process and impede prospects of landing a job! Nothing good can come from something bad if negativity and fear drive the emotional process.

If you face your fears and adversities in a courageous and positive manner, you can make the best of any circumstance. The bottom line is that you have the power to control how you feel at any moment, no matter what the situation. For example, two women experience the ultimate pain, the death of a child by a drunk driver. Both women experience unbearable grief. One woman commits suicide and destroys her life and the lives of those she leaves behind. The other, Candy Lightner, forms Mothers Against Drunk Driving. What was the difference? The difference was mindset—how they managed or mismanaged their emotions!

"How"—the Missing Link

Like a world-class athlete, mindset, or attitude, determines outcome; emotions determine success, or a lack thereof. You can have superior skills, but if you don't show up to play emotionally, you'll lose! In most cases, underdogs win, not by having superior skills, but by having a bigger heart, a stronger character, and a positive, unstoppable attitude. So when job loss and career issues create situations and events that require you to be at your emotional best, how do you get there? In other words, when well-meaning people tell you to "think positive" in the midst of crisis and chaos, how do you do this? Or better yet, how do you alter your emotions so that you actually benefit from the predicament you face? You're challenged to "take the high road" when you lose a job or when the job campaign takes longer than expected. You're advised to turn adversity into opportunity and to make the best of a bad situation. But once again, the question is, how do you accomplish this? The material in this chapter teaches you how. But before we delve into the how, you must be aware of the "five musts" for changing your state of mind—for managing fear and negative emotions to successfully land the job you want quickly.

1. *You must want to change.* You must make the decision to change and have a deep-rooted desire to be in total command of your emotional state at all times.

2. *You must be committed to change.* Commitment means you'll pay the price to attain your goals. Commitment means that quitting is not an option and that you'll be relentless in pursuit of your objectives.

3. *You must employ massive discipline in order to change.* Discipline means doing what you don't want to do in pursuit of what you want to achieve. Discipline means being aware of how you feel—knowing when your emotions are not serving you. Discipline means mastering just a few of the techniques that will be introduced in this chapter so

you remain calm and in emotional control to achieve your workplace goals.

4. *You must embrace discomfort to ensure change.* Here's one of the more profound statements I'll make in this chapter: discomfort cures "dis-ease." Physical therapy might be uncomfortable, but it will cure the dis-ease of a possible relapse or prolonged recovery. Networking and investing more time and energy in attaining a new job might be discomforting at first, but it will cure the dis-ease of continued unemployment or a prolonged job campaign. Discomfort is a gift. It's complacency and procrastination that induce poverty of the mind and atrophy of the spirit and rob you of any chance of landing a good job quickly. Complacency impairs any chance of success, whereas discomfort opens new doors of opportunity.

5. *You must condition yourself to learn new techniques to achieve lasting change.* Once you've learned the disciplines of managing your emotions and approach your job and career challenges with a fearless and confident constitution, you must condition yourself to master the techniques so they become second nature. Consistent repetition of new concepts and ideas is a success strategy—in other words, learning and conditioning new habits. If you start to walk an hour a day to improve your health and increase your energy so you can work harder and smarter at landing a new job, you must condition this activity so it becomes a new habit. If you send out 15 résumés, contact five people in your network, and spend three hours online every day to secure a new job, this activity must become habitual so you give yourself a clear advantage over other qualified candidates in securing the best opportunities that await you.

The 10 Principles for Success

Before I introduce you to four powerful emotional channeling techniques, techniques that will enable you to remain upbeat, positive, and optimistic during difficult times, I want to first share with you the 10 principles for successfully obtaining a new job. Actually, these principles are not new. The truth is that most people simply need to be reminded of what they already know—concepts that have been around for ages. The good news is that you don't need to learn any new, complicated principles. You just need to master the ones you know but perhaps forgot or treat too casually.

The list of 10 principles that I have assembled here represents the critical philosophies and strategies for rapid employment—landing the job you want at the pay you deserve. Once you have a clear understanding of these 10 principles and commit to them, the emotional channeling techniques presented later in this chapter will work more effectively and at lightning speed to produce a courageous attitude that will result in a new and rewarding job!

And I need to point out here that you can't simply pick and choose which of the 10 principles you like and which you'd like to ignore. All 10 must be acknowledged and implemented with equal passion. Landing a job in a complex and competitive job market requires that you become skillful with all 10 principles.

PRINCIPLE #1 *Personal Responsibility: If It's Going to Be, It's Up to Me*

The two major causes of underachievement are blame and excuses. Sadly, few people seem willing to take personal responsibility these days. Taking responsibility means accepting any type of wind that might blow, knowing that it's not the wind but rather the set of the sail that makes the difference between unemployment and gainful employment, between remaining in a stressful job and securing the perfect job. Taking responsibility means that if it's going to be, it's up to me and no one else! Responsibility means going the extra mile with a smile, knowing that going the extra mile is the best investment you can make in yourself and your future. Taking personal responsibility means not taking the path of least resistance even though it's a seductive option, but paying any price needed to succeed.

Responsibility means being a proactive and supportive resource in your own job campaign. You have a choice. You can spend 95 percent of your time and energy on the problem, blaming, finding excuses, and griping that the world is unfair. Or you can take personal responsibility and invest 95 percent of your time and energy on the solution, pursuing your career objectives with passion and confidence, knowing only you can stand in the way of your own success.

PRINCIPLE #2 *Desire: Nothing Happens Without First a Dream*

Purpose is everything. Purpose, or what I call "the pull of the future," is a remarkable force that propels you to achieve. Being "on purpose" means you're willing to commit to your dreams, desires, and career goals. Commitment means that you'll never give up on your quest for a better life, no matter what obstacles stand in your way, because you're driven to succeed. As long as the flame of desire burns deep within you, you'll achieve whatever it is you want to achieve, because all new job opportunities are born from a burning desire. A burning desire creates inner drive, and when you're driven to land a new and exciting job, all sorts of opportunities will present themselves—quickly.

PRINCIPLE #3 *Faith: Where There's a Will, There's a Way*

Faith is that ethereal power of knowing that miracles are born from obscurity when you believe. Faith is a belief, or a feeling of certainty, that something good can be created even though it has yet to be determined when or how it will occur. The expression "I'll believe it when I see it" is actually not the success formula for rapid employment. The formula that will help you get the job you want at the pay you deserve—quickly—is the opposite: "I'll see it when I first believe it." You first have to believe you can secure your next job; then you will.

Faith can be the belief that a higher power will help be a catalyst for the manifestation of your career goals. Or faith can be the unconditional belief in yourself and those around you, the belief that you have the power to achieve your mission. In any case, faith is that intangible, positive energy needed to land a job in any job market. The "how" hasn't arrived in your mind yet, but you have faith that it will.

PRINCIPLE #4 A "Healthy" Character: Success Achievement Is Not Attracted by an Unhealthy Attitude

A healthy character means developing a positive outlook on life no matter what serious situation you're facing. Well-respected basketball coach John Wooden said, "Be more concerned about your character than your reputation. Your reputation is how others perceive you; your character is who you really are." Character means having a healthy, positive attitude in the wake of job loss, job transition, or any life challenge for that matter. Clement Stone said, "There is little difference in people, but that little difference makes a big difference. The little difference is attitude. The big difference is whether it is positive or negative."

A healthy character means having the ability to use the right, honest, constructive thought, action, or reaction with any person, situation, or set of circumstances. It allows you to build on hope to overcome the feeling of despair and discouragement. A healthy character gives you the mental power, a feeling of confidence and positive expectation, to achieve anything at any time no matter what obstacles you face. Anyone can maintain a good attitude when things are going well. It's when the going gets tough that a healthy character inspires the tough to get going. One of the best methods for developing a healthy character is to appreciate all that you presently have. Most people tend to focus on what they don't have rather than on the many gifts they actually possess. A healthy character comes from a sincere appreciation for all that you have today in pursuit of all that you want tomorrow.

PRINCIPLE #5 Discipline: Without Discipline, Nothing Is Possible

Discipline is the bridge between employment and unemployment, between underemployment and meaningful employment. Discipline means doing those things that others aren't willing to do and hanging in there long after everyone else has let go. Discipline is the foundation upon which all success is attained. An abundance of discipline leads to an abundance of job offers! In reality, you have one of two life-changing choices to make: to employ discipline today to achieve your job objectives or neglect to employ discipline at the expense of your goals.

Discipline leads to reward. Neglect leads to regret. The great Vince Lombardi said, "Discipline and mental toughness are many things and rather difficult to explain. Its qualities are sacrifice and self-denial, and most importantly, it's combined with a perfectly disciplined will that refuses to give in."

The key is to choose discipline over "easy." You don't get to the World Series or the Olympics by easy, and you don't become a successful sales professional, nurse, administrative assistant, or CEO by easy. There is no "easy button" for landing a job. There are two four-letter words that always result in success and rapid employment: *hard work*!

PRINCIPLE #6 *A Positive Sphere of Influence: Your Environment May Determine How Quickly You'll Land Your Next Job!*

Will Rogers may have said it best when he said that "the quality of life is often a result of the people in life you avoid." It's important to consistently assess the people you spend time with and determine if they are with you or against you in identifying, pursuing, and getting a new job or beginning a new career. A president of a corporation is affected by those people serving on the board of directors. The president of the United States is affected by advisors and those in the cabinet. World-class athletes and entertainers surround themselves with world-class coaches and advisors. You, too, must have a positive, high-energy, and world-class group of advisors to help you meet your job and career objectives. This sphere of influence can be made up of a support group, job coaches, therapists, family members, and friends. The primary criterion for membership in your positive sphere of influence is that all members must be supportive of you and your goals. No, they don't always have to agree with you. You want constructive debate! But when they don't agree, they must do so without being disagreeable or combative.

Remember, influence can be subtle, so you must always be aware and evaluate those people you spend time with on a regular basis. Once aware of your sphere of influence, you'll want to determine whom you need to spend more time with, whom you need to spend less time with, whom you need to meet and add to your sphere of influence, and whom you need to disassociate with, either partially or completely. Demand more of yourself and of those you spend time with. When the demands are high, you'll achieve a new job or a more lucrative opportunity swiftly and enjoy the process along the way.

PRINCIPLE #7 *Embrace Adversity and Struggle: Strengthen Your Achievement Muscles*

Who came up with the expression, "Get it right the first time?" Who gets it right the first time? In fact, we're not supposed to get it right the first time. Thomas Edison failed nearly 10,000 times trying to invent the lightbulb. Walt Disney was turned down hundreds of times in his attempts to finance Disneyland. Babe Ruth struck out twice as many times as he hit home runs. Babies don't walk the first time they try. You probably don't want to read this, but adversity is the catalyst for all success. Massive failure leads to massive success. It's exciting to know that in every adversity lies the seed of a major opportunity. Did you learn how to read the first time you were introduced to the alphabet? No, you struggled with it. Yet because of the struggle, you can read this book!

Can you begin to see that failure is a human-made illusion of a perfectly natural phenomenon? In actuality, there is no such thing as failure; struggle yes, failure no! The human experience requires that you struggle for anything meaningful in life because it's the only way you can appreciate anything. How can there be meaning to life without an appreciation for life? We've created a monster by creating the concept of failure. Failure doesn't exist except when the fear of trying inhibits or outright prevents any attempt to achieve your potential.

The following story best illustrates the natural phenomenon of struggle and why struggle is a critical component and necessary ingredient for rapid employment.

The Butterfly Story

The wise old man of the village held a cocoon in the palm of his hand.

"What's that?" the young boy asked.

"Why it's a cocoon," replied the wise man. "Inside is a caterpillar that spun this cocoon. And when he's ready, he'll turn into a wondrous butterfly and break out of the cocoon."

"Oh, can I have it?" asked the young boy.

"Of course," answered the wise man. "But first you must promise that you won't open the cocoon for the butterfly when he begins to break out. The butterfly must do it all by himself. Can you promise me that?"

The young boy agreed and took the cocoon home with him.

The next day, the cocoon began to tremble, and the butterfly fought hard to escape it. The young boy couldn't bear to watch the butterfly struggle, and after a short while, he broke open the cocoon to help the butterfly escape. The beautiful butterfly soared into the air and suddenly, and quite unexpectedly, plummeted to the ground... and died.

The boy returned to the village wise man, in tears, cradling the dead butterfly in his hand.

"Did you help the butterfly escape from the cocoon?" the wise man asked.

"Yes," replied the child.

"What you didn't understand," the wise man said, "was that the butterfly had to struggle in order to build strength in his wings. By working hard to get out, the butterfly was building muscles that he needed in order to fly. By trying to make it easier for him, you actually made it harder for him, in this case, impossible, to fly. You killed him with good intentions."

So when you experience a so-called failure, don't view this as failure, but rather as an "achievement muscle-building" process. It's a process that will strengthen your resolve to transform your career much the same way a caterpillar transforms itself into a butterfly. The job campaign necessitates that you embrace struggle and constructively address adversity. When you do so, new opportunities will present themselves sooner than you'd think possible.

PRINCIPLE #8 *Fitness and Energy: Be Kind to Your Body; It's the Only One You Have*

Landing your new "right" job requires massive amounts of energy. Both physical and emotional well-being are important to assure rapid success. Two strategies for intensifying your energy level and over-all well-being are (1) proper nutrition and (2) consistent exercise. I strongly suggest you commit to developing a health and energy plan now and for the rest of your life. It can be as simple as taking a walk around the block, eating an apple a day, and reducing the intake of substances that impede fitness and vitality.

This is not the forum to provide an extensive set of guidelines for improving your health and energy. But there is clear, undeniable evidence, in the two-plus decades that I have coached job seekers and helped them land good-paying jobs, that health and energy played a pivotal role in their success. So let me share with you eight basic tips that will jump-start the process. These simple health and fitness tips are strategies that will help give you the energy and vivacity to land your next job.

1. Spend most of your time with health- and fitness-minded people. You can't believe the benefits of being around people who empower you to live a healthy and invigorating life.
2. Reduce your portions; don't overeat. When you're full, stop eating!
3. Drink more water and, as best you can, eliminate sodas.
4. Find periods every day to meditate, relax, and enjoy alone-time filled with positive and inspiring thoughts. Not only will you find a sense of calm; you'll also give yourself the time to come up with new ideas to meet your job and career goals. It's also an important way to recharge your emotional batteries just to be happy!
5. Eat more vegetables, fruit, and organic foods. You don't have to become a vegetarian. Just add more plant-based foods to your nutritional regimen.

6. Reduce your intake of dairy products and red meat.

7. Reduce your intake of caffeine, alcohol, and tobacco. When you decrease the poisons your body has to fight off, the more energy you'll have to invest in your job campaign.

8. Whenever you get the chance to move, move! Climb the stairs rather than take the elevator. Don't drive when you can walk. Don't look for the closest parking spot. And if you are restricted healthwise, work with your medical team to see what steps you can take to indulge in some form of exercise to improve your energy and fitness.

PRINCIPLE #9 *Acknowledge and Master Your Fears: Courage Is the Antidote to Fear*

As I've said from the get-go, fear is the main impediment to success. The primary enemy that stands in the way of getting your next job is fear. Fear is debilitating and incapacitating. That said, courage is the antidote to fear. Courage, according to Mark Twain, is "resistance to fear, mastery over fear, but not an absence of fear." That's what makes heroes—courage in the face of, not the absence of, fear. And that's what facilitates a successful and satisfying job campaign.

At this point, it's important that I acknowledge that the fear and pain of losing a loved one as well as losing a job is real, and it won't go away. Emotional and physical anguish, stress, and downright terror are permanent cast members on the stage of life. The goal is not to try and eliminate them, because they won't leave the stage! The objective, however, is to learn how to neutralize and effectively manage them. Landing your next job begins with the understanding that fear is ever present but will never be allowed to play a starring role. How to master fear management techniques is covered next in this chapter.

PRINCIPLE #10 *Take Action: The Miracle Principle*

All the planning in the world, all the processes, models, and strategies for rapid employment, means absolutely nothing unless fueled by action. The road to hell may be paved with good intentions, but the road to your next job is paved with activity and positive action. Action, driven by discipline, is what propels the process leading to an effective job campaign, to rapid employment. "Actions speak louder than words." Action is the miracle piece to all success achievement because when you take massive action, you'll get massive results.

Years ago, a teacher advised me to *make rest a necessity, not an objective.* Yes, you need to rest in order to revitalize and regain the energy required to take more action to achieve your goals. But once rested, common sense would dictate that even if you follow the first nine principles to a tee, without taking massive action, securing a new job quickly will be a major challenge. It's taking the right constructive action that will result in you landing your next opportunity in record-breaking time.

Emotional Channeling Techniques: Four Techniques for Managing Fear and Emotions During the Job Campaign

Emotional channeling techniques are specific strategies practiced by world-class athletes, entertainers, and business and political leaders to deal with and overcome fear, adversity, setbacks, and obstacles. These techniques inspire you to think positively during negative and difficult times. They'll help you remain calm and emotionally balanced when you are in the midst of job loss and when you face frustration during the job campaign. *Emotional channeling is personalized success conditioning.* It's the process of using specific strategies to consciously and proactively manage your state of mind on a continual basis to positively react to, and overcome, negativity in the wake of job loss, a prolonged job campaign, or any other career or life setback.

Awareness and Desire: The Keys to Successful Channeling

Emotional channeling requires both keen awareness and a burning desire: the awareness that you're in, or entering, a negative or fear-based emotional state (a bad attitude) and the desire to want to alter that state. If someone says something offensive to you, you must be aware that you're losing your cool, and you must have a desire to control your anger. Emotional channeling is only effective when you are aware that something is triggering a negative or fear-based emotional state. Once aware that you're on the verge of losing emotional control, you must have a desire to neutralize or outright eliminate that negative or fear-based emotion. If you continually raise your level of awareness, you'll continually improve your skills to properly manage your emotions and attitude. When this happens, you'll be in a better state of mind to conduct a flawless job campaign and land the right job quickly.

Below are four techniques that are highly effective when facing job loss and difficult career or workplace issues. Mind you, they won't make your problems go away! They will, however, allow you to get into a more empowered and positive mindset so you can quickly and effectively resolve them.

Emotional Channeling Technique #1: Courageous Questions

How do I raise the bar of dealing with my job loss and set an example for my family and friends, so that if they ever have to face a similar crisis, they'll do so with class and dignity? The Socratic method is a form of thoughtful inquiry where you explore the implications of your beliefs and those of others by asking high-quality questions to stimulate new thoughts and resolve issues and challenges. The powerful art of asking courageous, higher-quality questions is considered the oldest and most effective teaching strategy for fostering critical thinking and resolving job loss and job-related problems. Indeed, the quality of the questions you ask yourself and others, on a regular basis, determines the quality of answers you receive. The quality of answers you receive, in turn, determines the quality of emotions you experience and, thus, the speed at which you'll land a new job.

Socrates understood that the human brain is programmed to answer any question it's asked. For instance, if you ask the question, "Why me, God?" in the midst of a job loss, you might respond with, "I must have done something wrong to deserve this," or "I must not be very lucky and am just doomed to struggle my entire life." If you ask the question, "How will I ever make the same amount of money in my next job?" you'll probably answer with, "I must simply accept the reality that I'll never make what I'm worth again." These types of questions I call *destructive questions* because they result in further emotional conflict and anguish. Destructive questions seldom resolve anything in a constructive and positive manner.

If, on the other hand, you ask the question, "What lessons can I learn from losing my job?" you might respond with, "I'm learning courage and patience, and I'm setting the stage for a better job, better pay, and a better quality of life." If you ask the question, "Even though this is a highly competitive job market, what must I do to ensure that I make as much money as I made before?" you might answer with, "I must clearly identify my value and make sure I communicate my value in a powerful résumé, in all interviews, and throughout my job campaign. No doubt, if I am able to communicate my value, I'll earn even more than I did at my last job." These are called *courageous questions*. Courageous questions always lead to courageous answers that will inspire you to take the appropriate action to land a new job quickly. Courageous questions, if asked with high emotion, always result in high-quality, life-enhancing answers.

Tom Dempsey is widely known for his NFL record 63-yard field goal that he kicked in the final two seconds of a game to give his team, the New Orleans Saints, a 19–17 win over the Detroit Lions on November 8, 1970. But the real story is that Dempsey was born with half a right foot and no right hand. He had an unquenchable desire to be a professional football player, and as a result, his parents asked courageous and high-quality questions. Rather than ask, "How can you possibly play football in your condition?" Dempsey's parents asked a better question, "What can be done so Tom can pursue his dream?" As a result of asking courageous questions, an artificial foot and a modified shoe were made for him. Tom Dempsey's dream came true, and he became a professional football player and, at the time, broke the record for the longest field goal ever kicked.

Examples of Destructive and Courageous Questions

Courageous questions are questions that inspire answers to quell or significantly reduce fear and negativity to ignite the flame of hope and promote a successful job campaign. Consider the following:

Destructive question: Why does this always happen to me?
Courageous question: How can I use this to my advantage?

Destructive question: Why can't things be easier?
Courageous question: How can I become tougher and smarter?

Destructive question: When will things turn around for me?
Courageous question: How can I enjoy turning things
  around myself?

Destructive question: Will my spouse support me through
  this ordeal?
Courageous question: How can my spouse and I grow closer
  going through this?

Destructive question: Will I ever get a new job at the same pay?
Courageous question: What do I have to learn and whom do I
  have to meet to ensure I get a better job at a higher rate of pay?

Destructive question: How long will this job search last?
Courageous question: What action must I take to transform a job
  search into a powerful job campaign to land a job quickly?

Destructive question: What kind of burden will I be to
  my family?
Courageous question: How can I be an example to my family
  and make the best of a difficult situation?

Destructive question: How will I ever get through this?
Courageous question: How have I successfully dealt with this
  type of challenge in the past?

Below are just a few of the infinite questions that, if asked with
high emotion and a deep desire to seek out constructive answers, will
stimulate new thoughts to resolve your job and career challenges. By
asking courageous questions, your brain will come up with seemingly
miraculous answers so that you'll better manage negativity and fear. And
when you better manage negativity and fear, you'll be in a much better
state of mind to conduct your campaign and rapidly land your next job.

- How have others effectively dealt with this problem in the past?
- How do I turn this problem into an adventure and meet this challenge with a positive outlook?
- What can I learn from this, and how can I enjoy the process?
- What resources are available to me in the community that will assist me in getting a new job?
- What do I need to research to gain better control of my future?
- Whom can I recruit for my job campaign that will advise me and support my efforts in a positive way?
- How can I be a hero to myself and others by meeting this challenge head-on with confidence and self-respect?
- Am I spending more time on the solution than on the problem?
- Am I displaying leadership qualities to the members of my family so they can be proud of me?
- What do I have to read to make myself a more educated job campaigner?
- How can I make those I love more comfortable with my situation?
- Whom do I have to meet so I can achieve my goals quickly?
- What activities do I need to engage in to increase my energy to increase my chances of landing a job quickly?

When you begin to ask courageous questions, you'll challenge yourself to come up with life-changing, job-producing answers. When the right courageous questions are asked on a consistent basis, you'll come up with inspiring answers that will open doors to your next job opportunity. When feeling down, just say to yourself, "Ask a better question."

Emotional Channeling Technique #2: Focus Management

This technique is one of the most effective channeling techniques to induce constructive emotional shifts for identifying, pursuing, and landing your next job. Actually, it's one of the best techniques just to be happy in life! The primary concept behind focus management is to inspire you to voluntarily change your focus when you're in the midst of an emotional crisis or challenge. This technique works wonders simply by shifting your attention away from what's troubling you and focusing instead on something that's calming and comforting.

Focus Is About Attention—What You Pay Attention To

Human beings are strange creatures when it comes to what they focus on. Isn't it true that 10 great things can happen to you today along with just 1 bad thing, and in most cases, you'll go home and burden your family and yourself with that 1 bad thing while never even acknowledging the 10 good things? I know I've done that. So why is it that most people tend not to focus on the positive and fully engage themselves in the negative? The answer is simple. That's the way they were conditioned.

What's most exciting about this channeling technique is that you can easily recondition yourself to focus (or refocus) on those things that will help you reduce stress, overcome fear, and control your thoughts. You can live a high-quality life even if you are out of a job and struggling to pay the bills simply by paying attention to what you're paying attention to. By doing this, you can then refocus your thoughts on more positive aspects of your life to help you through the tough times. In other words, change your focus to change your life!

Focus Is Power

If you watch television and find that the constant bad news gets you down, you can continue focusing on the bad news and become more distraught, or you can shift your focus and change the station to one that is showing a comedy. You can go from a state of anguish to uncontrollable laughter—instantly!

The key to focus management is to first be aware of all the gifts you have currently in your life. When you lose a job, graduate from school and start to look for a job, don't win an interview, or face rejection after rejection during the job campaign, you have the power to focus on things that are going well in your life, things you have to be thankful for. When life isn't going the way you'd like and your emotions start to come unglued, you have the ability to refocus on the positive aspects of your life to offset those negative emotions. Are you focusing on the 7 percent unemployment rate or the 93 percent employment rate? Wouldn't you give anything for a 93 percent chance of winning the lottery? You see, when you refocus on the things that you are grateful for, the result will be happiness, hope, and peace of mind. With these inspiring emotions, you'll develop a winning attitude that will help set the stage to secure the job you want at the pay you deserve.

Joe DiMaggio had a father who consistently called him "good for nothing" throughout his youth. Why? Joe couldn't work in the family fish business because he got sick from the smell of fish. This didn't sit well with Joe's father, who thought Joe was just plain lazy. Even though his father's criticism created immeasurable pain, Joe refocused his attention, not on his father's anger and disappointment, but on Joe's love of baseball. By redirecting his focus, Joe DiMaggio was able to manage his emotions and become one of the greatest players to ever play professional baseball. And his father was his greatest fan!

So here's a question for you. Whom do you love most in the world? The next time you get into an emotional quagmire where you're focusing on something that upsets you, know that you have the power to instantly refocus your attention from that negative emotion and onto the people you love. What do you have to be grateful for? The next time you begin a typical temper tantrum, know that you have the power to instantly refocus your attention away from whatever set you off onto all that you have to be grateful for. It's that easy, just like switching from one television station to another! Once again, the technique does not make your problems go away. However it does place you in a better frame of mind to address and resolve your problems.

In the October 2007 edition of O, The Oprah Magazine, the cover headline read "How to Calm Down, Cheer Up; Oprah's Guide to Soothing Your Mind." Oprah suggests that during difficult times, "Distract yourself. Put on music and dance; scrub the bathtub spotless, whatever engrosses you." In other words, what Oprah is saying is, change your focus!

The essence of this emotional challenging technique is that you become acutely aware of what you're focusing on at all times. When you sense you're going into overwhelm or a fear-based negative emotional state, simply change your focus. The following is a short list of things you can focus on:

- The love of your family
- What you see
- What you smell
- What you feel
- What you hear
- What you taste
- Poetry
- Your pet
- Family photo albums
- Friendships
- Music
- Future dreams
- Happy memories
- A good movie
- A painting in your home
- Hobbies and interests
- Volunteer work
- Your good health
- A good book
- You live in the land of opportunity

When you begin to notice what you pay attention to most of the time, you'll realize how many gifts and blessings you simply take for granted. And when you change your focus and begin paying attention to all that you have to be grateful for, you'll also begin to focus on new ideas and creative solutions that will open doors to a myriad of opportunities.

Emotional Channeling Technique #3: Reference Validation

Reference validation is a technique where you compare your situation to that of others who have successfully dealt with and overcome what you are currently experiencing. By doing so, you find strength and hope and learn specific strategies and concepts used by others so you too can effectively work through and resolve the issues you have. Reference validation instills a feeling of certainty and a feeling of confidence because someone else or a group of people have successfully overcome similar adversities and challenges that you now face.

A support group is a good example of reference validation. People in a support group share their experiences with one another. They gain strength and hope by validating that they too can effectively deal with the challenge at hand. The Workforce System has established One-Stops (American Job Centers) and offices throughout the country where former out-of-work employees address groups of current out-of-work employees. The former out-of-work employees share their experiences and strategies that led to new jobs. Most educational institutions have career resource centers that offer similar services to those offered by One-Stops, and there are many job clubs available that provide needed support introducing former job seekers who share their success stories. Possibly you have the loving support of your family and friends while you work through your career and job issues, but still they don't seem quite able to understand how you really feel or don't have the answers you need. By attending a job-support group, you'll find that the shared experiences of others will serve to give you hope, confidence, and strategies needed to land a job quickly.

A Little League baseball coach noticed that many of his young players got angry and threw their bats in disgust after striking out. The coach sat the players down and told them that Babe Ruth hit over 700 home runs. He also pointed out that Babe Ruth also struck out over 1,300 times! The coach explained that Babe Ruth didn't throw his bat. He just returned to the dugout to think about what he had to do differently the next time in order to hit a home run. He told the boys that it took two strikeouts for Babe Ruth to hit one home run. From that moment on, whenever a player struck out, he calmly walked back to the dugout to think about what he had to do the next time in order to get a hit. The coach was able to help change the negative emotional state and subsequent behavior (bat throwing and temper tantrums) by providing an example the boys could relate to. They had a new positive frame of reference to better deal with their unsuccessful attempts.

A success coach worked with Jason, a 17-year-old boy whose father violently and unexpectedly committed suicide. His mother hired the coach to help because Jason, a high school varsity basketball player, stated that all his dreams had died when his father died. The coach told Jason that dreams were meant to come true and that people can achieve their dreams if they are committed to them, regardless of circumstances and tragic events. The coach shared with Jason a story about a kid named Larry, a basketball player who wanted to become a professional. But like Jason, something happened to Larry that could have made this lifetime dream impossible. Larry's father also committed suicide. Now the coach had Jason's attention. He explained to Jason that Larry had come to a crossroad in his life and had two choices. He could give up on his dream of becoming a professional basketball player, or he could work hard to make the NBA and dedicate his success to his father. Larry decided on the latter, and just a few years later, Larry Bird signed the largest rookie contract in the history of the NBA and became one of the game's greatest players. The coach gave Jason a new reference he could relate to. Once Jason understood that someone else had overcome a similar tragedy, this provided him with something that had been missing since his father's death—hope! Jason now had a new, powerful frame of reference to use to pursue his dreams.

Reference validation requires that you become a student of biographies, life events, and history and that you even recall your own personal situations and those of family members and friends. When you become aware of a negative or fear-based emotional shift or you experience a situation that begins to overwhelm you, you can immediately reference someone else who met and overcame a similar problem so you too are inspired to do the same.

To drive the point home, here's one last anecdote. And as a matter of fact, this person's story is legendary. He wanted a job, and that job was to become president of the United States. His business failed in 1831. He was defeated in his run for the Illinois State Legislature in 1832. His second business failed in 1833. He suffered a nervous breakdown in 1836. He was defeated in his run for Illinois House Speaker in 1838 and for his run for Congress in 1843. He was elected to Congress in 1846 but lost renomination in 1848. He lost his bid to the U.S. Senate in 1854, for vice president in 1856, and again for the U.S. Senate in 1858. Finally, in 1860, Abraham Lincoln was elected president of the United States. If Lincoln can do it, you can do it!

When frustration and emotional anguish test your will when you lose a job or are struggling to secure a new one, seek out references to cling to, much like a life preserver. Maybe you, a friend, or a family member has gone through job loss or a prolonged job campaign in the past, where you have references close to home on how best to get "back to work." Oftentimes you don't need to look far to find references to help guide you in a productive manner.

Emotional Channeling Technique #4: Humor Integration

We even have an expression for it: *laughter is the best medicine*. Faye was unexpectedly let go from her job. She was devastated and fearful.

But she never lost her sense of humor. When asked what her occupation was a week after her termination, she responded that she was a job campaign engineer.

Humor can change the way you feel in an instant, if you seek it out. Many times, in the midst of fear or anguish, someone says a funny one-liner, and it breaks the ice for everyone else. Just by asking the question, "What's funny about this?" you can change your emotions and how you feel, instantly. My favorite character on *Saturday Night Live* was loudmouthed Roseanne Roseannadana played by Gilda Radner. Everything about Gilda Radner, from her quick wit to her wide grin, just cracked me up. To this day, she is, and will always be, my favorite comedian. So, like millions of others, I was truly saddened when I learned that Gilda was diagnosed with ovarian cancer back in 1986. Remember, now, that the loss of a loved one (or good friend) and the loss of a job result in very similar emotions, so cancer affects our physical and emotional well-being in much the same way that joblessness does.

Back to Gilda. Being a comedian, she used humor to deal with her own runaway fears and negative emotions. She used a unique and creative method of humor integration by writing a book entitled *It's Always Something*. The book was a story about her life and her battle with cancer. She wrote that she began writing her book with a working title, *A Portrait of the Artist as a Housewife*. Originally the book was going to be a collection of stories on comical topics such as her toaster oven and her relationships with plumbers, mail carriers, and delivery people. But life dealt her a more complicated story. Cancer is not comical, but Gilda was a comedian, and even cancer couldn't stop her from seeing the humor in what she experienced. So she changed the subject matter and shared what she called a seriously funny book, one that confirmed her father's favorite expression about life... "It's always something."

In a seriously funny way, Gilda analyzed and evaluated her disease, torment, and fear. There were passages in the book where she was full of hope when she received good news about her remission. She went into comical detail about certain procedures she had to endure and about how she reacted when she lost her hair from chemotherapy. By using humor in her writing, Gilda managed to put a positive spin on a very bad situation.

Gilda Radner wrote her book with the reasonable expectation that she could control the ending. She could not. She died in May 1989 at the age of 42. But Gilda was fearless in her quest to deal with and overcome cancer, and she used humor to make the most out of every day she lived.

I totally agree that conducting a job campaign is a serious undertaking and should be treated as such. But there must be pockets of comic relief to help ease the tension and to stay healthy physically, mentally, and emotionally—for you and those you care for. Keep humor alive by reading funny books, watching funny movies, and enjoying a few laughs with family members and friends.

Humor is important because it fights off cynicism, pessimism, and a feeling of hopelessness. In 1964 Dr. Norman Cousins was diagnosed with a crippling and extremely painful inflammation of his body known as ankylosing spondylitis, a progressive degenerative disease. Dr. Cousins experimented with laughter to alter his body chemistry to be in a healing mode. He systematically watched *Candid Camera* classics and Marx Brothers films and read books like E. B. White and Katharine White's *Subtreasury of American Humor* and Max Eastmann's *The Enjoyment of Laughter*. He later wrote, "I made the joyous discovery that ten minutes of genuine belly laughter had an anesthetic effect and would give me at least two hours of pain-free sleep." He recovered from this condition and spent the next 20 years teaching about the merits of laughter and humor in healing and spent the last 10 years of his life doing clinical research at UCLA Medical School and established the Humor Task Force.

As you face your battle with joblessness and career-related issues, know that a dose of humor will go a long way in helping you achieve your goals and objectives. Being out of a job temporarily is not a terminal disease. It's 100 percent curable! And I've discovered that a few chuckles along the road to your next job will go a long way in helping you get there sooner rather than later. Shared laughter is a significant emotional channeling technique that says, "I am not defeated; I have a fighting spirit. So let's share a laugh or two and make the journey an enjoyable one."

Summarizing Emotional Channeling

Winston Churchill said that the natural state of the human experience is that of battle. From the moment we're conceived, we battle to survive and thrive. The key, I think, is to learn how to battle better and enjoy the good times as well as the challenging times. Just like a symphony, life has its high happy notes, and its sad low notes, and even its angry clash of the cymbals. We don't go to the symphony to enjoy just the high, happy parts of the performance. We sit and embrace the low and sad parts as well. This is what makes up the symphony, and this is what makes up life.

I, like you, was born without an owner's manual. Every day, I seek to find new answers to age-old questions in an effort to become a better warrior of life. It's been said that the greatest fear in life is not death. The greatest fear is what dies inside us while we live. So when negative and fearful emotions affect you in your pursuit of landing a new job, master the art of battling life and career issues better. You can do this by asking more courageous questions to come up with innovative and life-changing answers. Manage your focus, and focus mostly on what you have rather than on what you don't have. Use gratitude as a platform to achieve your job and workplace goals. Seek out others who have successfully overcome what you are facing, and determine what they did to achieve success. Then do the same. And finally, never lose your sense of humor. It really is the best medicine that will keep you calm and in control while you seek out and land your next employment opportunity.

STEP 1 SUMMARY

- Develop a fearless attitude as a first step in quickly landing a new job. Become an educated, enthusiastic, and confident campaigner to enable you to recover from job loss or to land a new job in competitive job markets.
- Change how you think about a job search—look at it as an easy five-step process that is a well-planned and well-executed campaign.

- Allow yourself to be uncomfortable, as complacency and comfort are not catalysts for constructive change. It is discomfort that cures dis-ease.
- Take personal responsibility for your future. Don't blame others or provide excuses. Adopt the belief that if it's going to be, it's up to me!
- Invest 95 percent of your time and resources on the solution, not the problem.
- Commit to identifying a meaningful goal, as all success is born out of a burning desire to achieve success.
- Have faith. Faith is a feeling of certainty, a feeling that something good can be created even though it has yet to be determined when or how it will occur.
- Work on building and improving your character. A healthy character comes from a sincere appreciation for all that you have today in pursuit of all that you want tomorrow.
- Employ massive amounts of discipline. Discipline means doing what you don't want to do to get the job you want at the pay you deserve.
- Surround yourself with positive and empowering people. In most cases, the people you associate with determine how quickly you'll land a new job.
- Accept and embrace adversity and failure. Know that setbacks, obstacles, and failures are a necessary component to all success achievement.
- Work hard on your fitness and health. Landing a new job requires a lot of energy. Eat well and exercise regularly to give yourself the vibrancy you'll need to secure a new, rewarding job.
- Take massive action. Action, driven by discipline, is what propels the process of getting a new job quickly.
- Ask courageous questions. Asking high-quality questions stimulates new thoughts. New, more empowered thoughts will lead to rapid employment.
- Manage your focus. Focus on what you have to be grateful for and what's going well in your life. If you focus on the negative, you'll get negative results. If you focus on the positive, you'll get

positive results. What you focus on determines your mindset and how quickly you obtain a new job.

- Reference others who have successfully dealt with and overcome what you are currently experiencing. By doing so, you find strength and hope. And learn specific strategies and concepts used by others so you too can effectively work through and resolve your employment issues.
- Use humor to gain emotional balance in your life while you pursue a new job. Laughter is the best medicine, not only for health issues, but for all life's adversities including job loss and employment matters.

2

DEFINING YOUR GOAL

Identify Workplace Goals
That Inspire Your Life

Envision a boat with an engine on the back. Now picture the boat as your life and the engine as your job or career. The purpose of the engine is to power the boat to go where you want the boat to go and to do all the things you want to do. Metaphorically speaking, the boat is your life, and the engine is your career. The purpose of your job is to empower your life so you can achieve all that you want to achieve in life. The problem is that most people spend the first 20 years or more of their lives in school preparing how to earn a living, not how best to design and live their lives.

Two Important Questions

To better understand the problem, we need only go back to that infamous question we ask youngsters early on. During their youth, children are asked over and over again, "What do you want to be when you grow up?" As a result, throughout your entire life, your identity is directly related to what you do in the workplace, not what you do in life or who you become as a person.

So you begin your life's journey on the academic assembly line in pre-school or kindergarten and then, for the next 12 to 16 years or more, you prepare for one thing—getting a job. Most of your time in academia is spent on the engine of the boat, not the boat itself. And truth be known, the question "What do you want to be when you grow up?" is so ingrained into your being, you wind up spending your entire life seeking that elusive answer to this question, even at the age of 50 or 60! I constantly have people come up to me and ask, "How do I determine my dream job?" I answer the question by asking two of my own: (1) "What do you want to get out of life?" and (2) "What do you want to give back to life?" In other words, what are your life ambitions? Who do you want to become? What do you want to own? Whom do you want as friends? What do you want to achieve and accomplish? What do you want to give back to your community? How do you want to contribute to making this world a little bit better place when you leave than when you arrived? And how do you want to be remembered?

Survey after survey confirms that somewhere between 75 and 90 percent of workers are uninspired with, or downright dislike, their jobs. When questioned, a good majority of people claim they would quit their jobs if they won the lottery. Most people feel that they are under-paid, overworked, and/or underappreciated in the workplace. However, those few people who seem genuinely happy and successful at their jobs are those who acknowledge that they work at jobs and careers that inspire their life's dreams and ambitions. They understand that the key to living a full and rewarding life is to first identify what kind of life would be considered full and rewarding. They know how they want to live, what kind of person they want to become, and what dreams and desires they want to pursue and achieve. Simply stated, those people who are enjoying life's journey, regardless of the challenges they face along the way, know their values (what makes them happy) and have exciting goals they wish to achieve. Then, once defined, they identify career and job opportunities that will be a catalyst for attaining the life they have designed for themselves.

When the Vision Is Clear, You'll Pay the Price

Every ambition has its price. The truth is, you'll pay almost any price if your ambitions and goals are inspiring ones. Said differently, you'll do whatever it takes when you are passionate about and committed to your goals. And if you don't know what your life goals and ambitions are, you might simply consider becoming passionate about defining them.

Here's a fact that should grab your attention. If you don't have ambitions and goals of your own, you'll be destined to spend your entire life working hard to help others achieve their ambitions and goals at the expense of your own. And goals that are not clear are clearly not goals. What cannot be identified cannot be attained. So the starting place for helping you identify your next job or career opportunity is not by determining what kind of job you want to work at, but rather by determining what kind of life you envision for yourself and your family. Once that vision is clear and you are jazzed about attaining it, meaningful job and career options will present themselves because you will be excited and motivated to seek them out.

The Four Universal Truths

There are four universal truths related to determining what workplace opportunities would best provide you with the life you want:

1. As I noted previously, *there is no magic pill*. If there were, the majority of people would be taking the pill and living for the week, not just the weekend.

2. *Vocational tests are not effective*. If tests were useful, most people would be graduating from high school and college knowing precisely what job and career options would best inspire their lives. If vocational tests actually worked, it would stand to reason that 75 to 90 percent of the working population would enjoy what they do rather than the other way around.

3. *If you are not working diligently on identifying what constitutes a quality life for you and your family, odds are no one else is working on this for you.* And if you are putting this off or ignoring what constitutes a quality life for you and your family, know that the *law of ignoring* will surely kick in. The law of ignoring says that whatever you ignore will, most likely, get worse in time. If you want to live life

on your terms and secure a job that provides the life you want, you have to make it happen.

4. *You must make time and enjoy the process of introspection.* You must take the time to think, reflect, contemplate, and indulge in personal introspection. A Zen expression says that *if you're not willing to go within, you'll have to go without!* Breakthroughs and new ideas normally don't present themselves when you're watching television or engaged in diversionary activities such as texting on your smartphone. You need to find a tranquil and peaceful setting where you can allow your thoughts and emotions to soar. Isn't it interesting that one of the major abilities that characterize human beings is the ability to think? Yet most people go to bed with the same thoughts they awoke with. *How can you create anything new tomorrow with the same thoughts you had yesterday?* You must take time out of every day to think, to engage in self-reflection. It takes only one new thought to manifest a life-changing breakthrough, one idea to go from broke to fortune, and one idea to go from unemployed to happily employed. But that one new thought won't happen by chance; it will happen as a result of investing time to journey within.

The Five Components to Identifying Meaningful Career Goals

In 1992 when I was fired by one of my best friends, I was 39 years old and going through a serious midlife crisis. I knew I had the potential to be successful. I worked hard; I had a good education and was raised in a loving family. I grew up in a wonderful town and had many close friends. So how was it that with all the gifts that had been bestowed upon me, I was a satellite in the wrong orbit at age 39? The answer, I discovered, was that I wasn't taught the five components to identify the kind of job and career that would inspire me or my life. Once I learned these five components, my life changed almost instantly!

This chapter will introduce you to the five components that turned my life and career around. And they have also worked successfully for thousands of people I have shared them with over the years. Each one requires specific work assignments that I will ask you to do. And as I lead you through these five components, I'll share with you the assignments I completed that helped turn my entire life around. This way you will see how I went from clueless to clarity in discovering what career would best inspire and enrich my life. The five components are:

1. Identify your signature life values.
2. Identify your signature career values.
3. Acknowledge activities and environments that interest you.
4. Evaluate current market opportunities.
5. Consider the four global options using the Circle of Options model (provided later in the chapter) to determine your long- and short-term career goals.

Component #1: Identify Your Signature Life Values

A value is something that makes you happy! Values come from the heart and are immutable at the moment. Yes, they may change tomorrow, a month from now, or a year from now. But at this moment, *your signature values are something you feel so strongly about, they can't be changed or compromised.* In fact, they determine how happy you are at any moment in your life. And the word *signature* means that you have a hierarchy (a prioritized list) of values that are yours and yours alone. The only way you can find joy in life and in your career is to know what your signature values are and then to work hard living harmoniously with them. For instance, if you value health and are not healthy physically or emotionally, you can't be happy. If you value financial independence and are broke, you can't be happy. If you value a loving relationship and you are in a toxic and unhealthy one, you can't be happy. If you value peace of mind but experience constant stress, you can't be happy.

The challenge for most people is that they simply aren't aware of their signature values. As strange as this may be, most people don't know what really makes them happy! When you drive a car and are holding the steering wheel, doesn't the steering wheel move back and forth continually while the car is in motion even when you are going straight? The reason the steering wheel is always moving is because the car is always trying to go off course. If you don't continually move the steering wheel, you'll crash! The same is true for your life and your career. If you don't continually control the values that determine your happiness, you'll crash emotionally! Every emotion you feel, every decision you make, and every action you take is guided, in large part, by your value system—your signature values. And here's what's exciting about your values. Though you may have 20, 30, or more values, *there are only about 6 to 8 that make up 90 percent of your happiness*. This means that when you identify your top 6 to 8 values and place them in a hierarchy of importance, you will then know precisely what makes you happy. With this heightened level of self-awareness, you can then begin the process of working toward living your life in harmony with your signature values. And when you live life and work at a job that is aligned with your values, you can't believe the joy you'll get out of every day! Life becomes an exciting adventure inclusive of what good things and not-so-good things happen along the way. On the other hand, when you live life in conflict with your values, you'll be constantly stressed out and unhappy. Life will be a daily struggle.

So this first assignment will help you determine your *signature life values*. As an example for you to associate with, I've provided you with the assignments I completed after being fired back in 1992. Use me as an example, but understand that my signature values are mine. You have to determine yours because that's the only way you can be happy and live a fulfilling life and work at a meaningful job. And when you work on this first assignment, please allow yourself to feel your values. This exercise requires very little thinking. It does, however, require you to open your heart and emotions to what's really important to you. Do not spend time judging or analyzing your values. When you intellectualize your values, you allow your head to get in the way of your heart, and you'll wind up confused and in conflict. The key here is to allow your heart (your feelings) to surface. When you make intellectual decisions that are in conflict with your true feelings, you'll make poor decisions and wind up saying, "My heart's not in this anymore." Unhappiness and frustration will prevail. The message here is that you must trust your feelings and emotions and give yourself the gift of knowing those six to eight things that make you happy.

How do you determine your values? You do so by asking yourself the following question: "What's most important to me in my life that will make me happy and that will significantly enrich the quality of my life?"

Plan to invest at least two to three hours reflecting on and answering that question. Ideally, you should be in a peaceful, relaxed, and empowering environment. Get fired up and allow no interruptions. Let yourself feel all those aspects of life that would make you happy, provide meaning, and bring joy to you and others. Then write them down. And yes, you might experience some initial fear when doing this because your conditioned reaction might be "How will I ever achieve this?" At this time, the *how* is not important. Just identify what makes you happy because when the *desire* is clear, the *how* will inevitably show up. We know this to be true by the expression "Where there's a will, there's a way."

Below are my values from 1992. Keep in mind that I hadn't a clue, at age 39, what I wanted to be when I grew up or what would make me happy in life; I was just sleepwalking through each day! Through this process I discovered the answer. And so can you! Be sure and brainstorm (heartstorm, actually) your values, not mine. Recall times when you were the happiest. What made you happy? Think of times when you weren't so happy. What would have made you happy during those times? Consider all this, and just write down your thoughts without analyzing or judging them.

Assignment: Stop and invest quality time answering the question, "What's most important to me in my life that will make me happy and that will significantly enrich the quality of my life?" In addition to listing my life values back in 1992, I've provided a detailed list of values to help you to come up with your own.

Your Life Values. What's most important to me in my life that will make me happy and that will significantly enrich the quality of my life?

Jay's values in 1992

Health, freedom, a loving relationship, financial independence, family, friends, adventure, tranquility, golf, significance, time, respect, a nice home, a meaningful career, integrity, spirituality, travel, achievement, contribution, the power to influence, personal growth, tolerance, honesty, compassion, healthy competition, a Rolex watch, world travel, and a 150-foot yacht.

A Partial List of Life Values

Health and fitness	Independence	Love
Hard work	Leisure activities	Financial freedom
Security	A loving family	Good friends
Exciting activities	Peace of mind	Peace on earth
Helping others	Sports	Respect
Honesty	Time	Trustworthiness
Spirituality	Patience	A nice home
A good job	Travel	Achievement
Community giving	Leadership	Personal growth
Compassion	Creativity	Loyalty
Acceptance	Comfort	Competency
A sense of humor	Courage	Control
Order	Kindness	Wisdom
Persistence	Thoughtfulness	Silliness
Sexuality	Recognition	

Did you take the time to identify *your* life values? If you are reading this now, I assume you have taken the time and responded to the question and now have your own list of values. Did you discover any surprises or breakthroughs? When I created my list in 1992, I was most surprised by my values of significance and the power to influence because I wasn't even aware of them! And because I was living my life without these two values, this caused quite a bit of pain in my life. So I hope you invested quality time determining what makes you happy, because if you don't know what brings you joy, how can you ever expect to be happy?

Your Top Eight Values and the Hierarchy

Now it's time to look at your list of life values and identify your top eight. Then you will prioritize them in the order of importance that naturally makes you happy. In other words, when you look at your hierarchy, it should feel great! Prioritizing your values or placing them in a hierarchy allows you to better understand why you think the way you think, feel the way you feel, and act the way you act. Though all eight values are extremely important, some are a little more important than others. For instance, my eyesight is a little more important to me than my hearing, but that doesn't mean my hearing isn't important. By realizing this, I understand now why I'd be a bit more excited about going to a movie than a concert. I now understand why, when someone gives me directions, I prefer to see a map rather than be told where to go. If I know my hierarchy of values, I'll make better decisions because I know better what to base those decisions on.

If finding a loving relationship and securing a new job are values that are important to you, but deep down in your heart, a loving relationship is a bit more important than securing a new job, you'll probably allocate more of your energy and resources to finding a loving relationship than you will to securing a new job. Your signature values represent your personal guidance or navigational system that steers your emotions and your life. If you live in harmony with your signature values, you'll find a deep sense of happiness and personal fulfillment. If you don't, you open yourself up to constant pain, stress, and conflict.

Assignment: In the next exercise, you will prioritize your top eight signature values. Keep in mind that all eight are very important. But your #1 value will be a bit more important to you than your #2 value, and your #2 value will be a bit more important than your #3 value, and so on. Once your values are in the proper hierarchy, you will have identified your signature life values. Then you can begin to live your

life and make decisions based on this hierarchy. It's the only way you
can live a happy, joyful, and fulfilling life.

**What are the eight most important values that will make me happy
in life and the hierarchy of importance that constitutes my signature
values?**

1.   (   )   5.   (   )
2.   (   )   6.   (   )
3.   (   )   7.   (   )
4.   (   )   8.   (   )

Jay's hierarchy of values in 1992
1. A loving relationship   (   )
2. Freedom   (   )
3. Financial independence   (   )
4. A meaningful career   (   )
5. Significance   (   )
6. The power to influence   (   )
7. Family and friends   (   )
8. Health   (   )

I expect that you have completed this assignment and now have
your life values in a hierarchy of importance, just as I listed mine
above back in 1992. Your emotional state and the actions you take in
life are determined by how well you live according to your priority or
hierarchy of values. So once again, I ask the question, did you discover
any surprises or breakthroughs? When I put my values in the hierarchy
above, I was most surprised that my values of a loving relationship
and freedom came ahead of financial independence and a meaningful
career, even though I was broke at the time and had no clue what I
wanted to do for a living. But you see, I didn't analyze or judge my
hierarchy. This is how I felt. I didn't "intellectualize" or question my
feelings and emotions!

Grade Your Values

Now that you know what makes you happy and in the hierarchy that feels right to you, it's time to evaluate how happy you presently are with each value. This is an exercise where you CAN use your intellect, your brain. You will notice parentheses following each value. Once you have your values listed in the correct hierarchy (your signature life values), go back and grade each one (I used an A–F grading system) based on how you feel you are currently living your life in harmony with that value. As you can see by how I graded my values back in 1992, my life was somewhat of a challenge, to say the least!

1. A loving relationship	(F)
2. Freedom	(B)
3. Financial independence	(D)
4. A meaningful career	(F)
5. Significance	(C)
6. The power to influence	(C)
7. Family and friends	(C)
8. Health	(C)

Analyze Your Grades, Not Your Values

After grading my values, I reviewed and analyzed my grades. As I did, I realized that there were things I could do immediately to improve some of my grades. I could work on my health immediately by eating better and exercising more. That would instantly improve my grade from a C to a B. I could immediately improve my relationships with family members and friends just by making a more concerted effort to do so. I could instantly bring that C up to a B just by staying in touch with them more because *I had total control over that*! And the power to influence could easily become an A if I used the power to influence myself to work harder than ever to achieve a happier, more meaningful life. In fact, I had a breakthrough with my power-to-influence value: I got excited about using the power to influence to define and achieve a purposeful life and career.

Though nothing tangible had yet occurred, I felt an adrenaline rush because I felt genuine hope and anticipation. My two lowest grades were my #1 value (a loving relationship) and my #4 value (a meaningful career). But I had another breakthrough! I discovered that if I could improve the grades for my #6, #7, and #8 values, I'd have a much better "report card," and more importantly, I'd be much happier. The breakthrough came when I discovered that if I were happier, I'd be a lot more motivated to address my relationship and career challenges.

So I made the decision to be happier and changed my grades. Compare my original grades, with attention to life values #6, #7, and #8, with my new, more empowering grades:

Jay's initial grades

1. A loving relationship	(F)
2. Freedom	(B)
3. Financial independence	(D)
4. A meaningful career	(F)
5. Significance	(C)
6. The power to influence	(C)
7. Family and friends	(C)
8. Health	(C)

Jay's new, revised grades

1. A loving relationship	(F)
2. Freedom	(B)
3. Financial independence	(D)
4. A meaningful career	(F)
5. Significance	(C)
6. The power to influence	**(A)**
7. Family and friends	**(B+)**
8. Health	**(B)**

The power behind this exercise is to first identify your signature life values and then to evaluate them and revise them so they accurately reflect how things really are. You do this by evaluating, grading, and then upgrading or revising your level of happiness for each of your values when possible. In other words, you can change your beliefs to find a higher degree of happiness to better address your challenges. I certainly had 100 percent control over my health and my relationships with family members and friends, and yet I gave myself a C. By realizing I was not controlling what I could control—like my health, my relationships with family members and friends, and my power to influence—I immediately improved my grades (changed my beliefs) and seized the power I always had to influence myself to be happier. By realizing this and being genuinely happier in these areas, I could better focus on and address my two major challenges—my relationship and career issues.

If you are like most people, you'll find that, like me back in 1992, you are not controlling those aspects of your life you actually have control over and aren't fully appreciating those things that are actually going well in your life. Once you make some adjustments in how you manage your happiness by changing your beliefs and revising the actual happiness levels for those values you are currently undervaluing, you too can constructively and enjoyably address your major issues, such as landing a job or improving your career.

Assignment: At this time, please return to your hierarchy of eight signature life values and grade them. Once graded, go back and reevaluate each one and ask yourself if you can create a newfound level of happiness by revising and improving some of your grades, just as I did. By doing so, you will find a greater level of happiness and achieve rapid results in those areas that need it most.

Values Will Shift and Change

Indeed, your life's values will constantly shift and change. If you find that special person and get married, you have a new value that will head toward the top of your hierarchy. If you have children and need to start saving for their college education, saving money may be a value that moves up your hierarchy while the values of adventure or leisure activities might slide down. If health is your #7 value and you are diagnosed with a serious health issue, health will, most likely, ascend from #7 to #1. Certainly getting healthy will supersede almost everything else on your list. Just like the steering wheel that continually moves back and forth to keep your car safely on the road, you must continually evaluate and "steer" your values (your happiness) so you can keep your life on track. This means you must review and revisit your signature life values on a regular basis.

Component #2: Identify Your Signature Career Values

You will now use the exact same strategy that you used to determine your signature life values to identify and prioritize your signature career values. You will ask the same question but substitute the word *career* for *life*: "What's most important to me in my career or job that will make me happy and that will significantly enrich the quality of my life?"

Once again, you will want to invest at least two to three hours on this assignment. Below I share with you my career values back in 1992 to use as an example. I remind you again that my signature career values are, most likely, different from yours. So be sure to spend quality time identifying what makes you happy in a job or career because this is your future you are designing!

Assignment: Stop and invest quality time answering the question, "What's most important to me in my career or job that will make me happy and that will significantly enrich the quality of my life?" In addition to listing my specific career values back in 1992, I've provided a detailed list of career and job values to help you to come up with your own. Recall times when you were the happiest in a job or career. What made you happy? Think of times when you weren't that happy. What would have made you happier during those times? Think about all those things that would constitute the perfect job or work environment and just write them down without analyzing or judging them.

Your Career Values. What's most important to me in my career or job that will make me happy and that will significantly enrich the quality of my life?

> **Jay's career values in 1992**
> Writing, creativity, diversity, freedom, training people, helping others, being an industry leader, multiple streams of income, financial independence, respect, set my own schedule, travel, the power to influence, personal growth, and healthy competition

A Partial List of Career Values

Competitive	Supervise others
Earn a lot of money	High social status
Job security	Artistic expression
Independence	Problem solving
Leadership	Improve the environment
Friendships	Advancement
Physical challenge	Location of work
Short commute	Fast-paced environment
Work alone	Work in teams
Work with information	Work with data
Work with ideas	Change society for the better
Flexible schedule	No weekend work
Contact with the public	Recognition
Minimal stress	Precision work
Invent or create	Learning new things
Variety and change	Constant challenge
Structure	Adventure and excitement
Honesty and integrity	Power or authority
A good boss	A reputable company
A big corporation	A small company
Travel	Help society

I hope you put quality time into this important assignment because you can't be happy in a job when you don't know what makes you happy. At this point, you should have a comprehensive list of your career values.

Assignment: Now, as you did with your life values, you'll want to identify your top eight career values and then place them in a hierarchy of importance. Remember, when you define your signature career values, you begin the almost miraculous process of taking control of your future because you will be crystal clear on what has to happen for you to be happy in your next job! Only then can you identify, pursue, and land a fulfilling job quickly and effectively... a job that will enrich your whole life!

What are the eight most important values that will make me happy in my career and the hierarchy of importance that constitutes my signature values?

1.	( )	5.	( )
2.	( )	6.	( )
3.	( )	7.	( )
4.	( )	8.	( )

Jay's hierarchy of values in 1992

1. Freedom   (F)
2. Helping others   (F)
3. Writing   (B)
4. Financial independence   (D)
5. Training people   (C)
6. Industry leadership   (F)
7. Creativity   (C)
8. Multiple streams of income   (D)

Grade Your Last Job(s)

Since this exercise will be pivotal in helping you define those qualities that will make you happy in your next job or career, I hope you put high-quality time and thought into this assignment. Did you come up with any breakthroughs? Did anything surprise you? When I put my values in the hierarchy above, I was most surprised that my top three out of four values were Fs and a D. And five of my eight values were either Fs or Ds. And as hard as I tried, I was unable to upgrade or revise any of them. That being said, I studied my hierarchy of career values and the grades I gave them. Then I thought to myself, "There's little wonder why I had no passion for my job and got myself fired." As I look back on that job, I realize that my good friend did me a big favor by firing me!

Assignment: Please return to your signature career values and grade them. Then go back and reevaluate them and ask yourself if you can create a newfound level of happiness by upgrading and improving some of your grades. By doing this, you can begin the process of addressing those other values that need to be addressed with a better attitude—a better perspective to help you select job or career options that inspire you.

Assignment: At this point, you should have identified both your signature life and signature career values. This will allow you to make high-quality decisions about future job and career options. Before we move on to Step #3, let's put your signature life and career values together for future reference just as I did.

Jay's Life and Career Values

Jay's eight life values

1. A loving relationship	5. Significance
2. Freedom	6. The power to influence
3. Financial independence	7. Family and friends
4. A meaningful career	8. Health

Jay's eight career values

1. Freedom	5. Training people
2. Helping others	6. Industry leadership
3. Writing	7. Creativity
4. Financial independence	8. Multiple streams of income

Your Life and Career Values

My eight life values

1.	( )	5.		( )	
2.	( )	6.		( )	
3.	( )	7.		( )	
4.	( )	8.		( )	

My eight career values

1.	( )	5.		( )	
2.	( )	6.		( )	
3.	( )	7.		( )	
4.	( )	8.		( )	

Component #3: Acknowledge Jobs and Industries That Interest You

When you explore new job and career options, you need only define (1) jobs that would interest you, that you are or could be qualified to do, and that are in harmony with your career and life values and (2) industries that interest you. The T-Bar model is a self-brainstorming tool to help you answer the question, "What do I want to do?" On one side of the "T," you'll list jobs. On the other, you'll list industries.

Example

POTENTIAL JOBS	POTENTIAL INDUSTRIES
1. Computer programmer	1. Healthcare
2. Sales professional	2. Entertainment
3. IT consultant	3. Sports
4. Trainer or technical trainer	4. Technology environments
5. Technical writer	5. High-end automotive
6. Technical troubleshooter	6. Music industry and venues
7. Animation or movie director	
8. Musician	

Assignment: Using the T-Bar model, complete your next assignment by writing down all the jobs and industries that would interest you. At this time, write down all the different jobs that you might enjoy on the left side of the T-Bar. On the right side, list all the potential industries you might be interested working in. Write everything down no matter how ridiculous it might seem at first. Be innovative, bold, and honest with yourself! You can always delete your ideas later. Consider those jobs and industries you have enjoyed in the past. Also, write down ones you've always dreamt about. What jobs or industries would turn you on? What jobs or industries would be so enjoyable that your weekdays would actually be more exciting than your weekends? Invest a good amount of time on this assignment and don't leave anything off this list. If an idea comes to you, write it down! When done, place the items in a hierarchy where the most exciting jobs and industries are atop the list. My list, from 1992, is below.

Jay's T-Bar in 1992

POTENTIAL JOBS	POTENTIAL INDUSTRIES
1. Writer	1. Sports
2. Trainer	2. Employment or job
3. Speaker or presenter	management
4. Marketing and	3. Motivation and empowerment
communications	4. Tourism
5. Manager	5. Business consulting
6. Adventure guide	

Now is the time for you to brainstorm your own list. (By the way, if you find that you need a comprehensive resource to further assist you, the U.S. Department of Labor has identified over 40,000 specific job titles that are available in its publication *Occupational Outlook Handbook*.)

Your T-Bar

POTENTIAL JOBS	POTENTIAL INDUSTRIES
1.	1.
2.	2.
3.	3.
4.	4.
5.	5.
6.	6.
7.	7.
8.	8.

Component #4: Evaluate Current Market Opportunities

No doubt, you'd certainly have a challenging time landing a job as a snowplow operator in Florida or getting a job as a pay-phone repair person at a time when almost everyone has a cell phone. But in virtually every type of job market, there are many job opportunities and almost unlimited ways to earn a good income. You just have to know what they are. Study the job market where you live or where you are seeking work. You must know what jobs and industries are hot and what ones are on the decline. I also suggest you research what opportunities are on the rise, because many lucrative income-producing jobs might not be traditional jobs but instead contract positions, entrepreneurial opportunities, or opportunities for combining multiple streams of income.

Conduct your own in-depth research online. Enter the keywords "growth industries," and specify your geographic area. Read newspapers, including the business section as well as the classified section. Pay attention to what's going on in your market; speak to businesspeople you might know or to professionals at the Workforce One-Stops (American Job Centers). Visit your local chamber of commerce and ask employees there what market opportunities are growing. Another source of market information can be provided by executive recruiters.

Invite an executive recruiter out to lunch and get his or her take on the job market. Ask everyone and anyone you can about what jobs are in demand, what companies are hiring, and what industries are expected to flourish. And once you have performed an in-depth study of your market, write down the top six to eight jobs and industries that currently provide the best opportunities.

In 1992 when I was fired from my job, the U.S. economy was just working its way out of a severe recession. The unemployment rate in Florida, where I lived, was 8.9 percent. Many industries that drove Florida's economy were struggling, including tourism, real estate, construction, finance, and food and beverage. I performed a detailed job market analysis and identified growth jobs and emerging industries. I've included them in the list below:

Jay's list of the top six to eight jobs and industries that provided the best opportunities in 1992	Your list of the top six to eight jobs and industries currently providing the best opportunities today
1. Medical sales and healthcare	1.
2. Résumé and employment counseling	2.
3. Transportation	3.
4. Distribution	4.
5. Import-export	5.
6. Personal health and fitness	6.
7. High tech, computer, and Internet	7.
8. Law enforcement and security	8.

Assignment: Your next assignment is to perform a job market analysis in your area so you know which specific jobs and industries to consider. Take time to perform the appropriate due diligence and gather information that will help you identify growth and emerging industries. This is also called *intelligence gathering*. Once you have completed this, you can better select the right job and industry for you. Then list the information in the spaces above.

Component #5: Know the Four Global Options Using the Circle of Options Model

At this point, you should have a considerable amount of information to help you make a decision about what new career direction would be best for you. When you know your life and career values, you have identified the jobs and industries you'd like to work in, and you have a grasp of current market opportunities, you can use this information to select viable career options like pieces of a puzzle. You may very well come up with both long- and short-term goals. For instance, you may decide that the long-term goal is to become an office manager for a medical practice. The short-term goal may be to secure a part-time job for six months while you take computer classes and a financial accounting class that will give you the added skills and qualifications needed to land a job as an office manager.

Assignment: At this time, you will put all the pieces to the career puzzle together in one place. This way, you'll have the information readily available so you can see the BIG picture in order to make BIG decisions. Please do this now!

Your Life and Career Values

My eight life values

1.
2.
3.
4.
5.
6.
7.
8.

My eight career values

1.
2.
3.
4.
5.
6.
7.
8.

Your T-Bar

POTENTIAL JOBS	POTENTIAL INDUSTRIES
1.	1.
2.	2.
3.	3.
4.	4.
5.	5.
6.	6.
7.	7.
8.	8.

Six to Eight Jobs and Industries That Currently Provide Employment Opportunities for You

1.   5.

2.   6.

3.   7.

4.   8.

Notes, reflections, and breakthroughs: Write down anything that comes to mind that is important or that might represent an "aha" moment.

Jay's Life and Career Values

Jay's eight life values

1. A loving relationship
2. Freedom
3. Financial independence
4. A meaningful career
5. Significance
6. The power to influence
7. Family and friends
8. Health

Jay's eight career values

1. Freedom
2. Helping others
3. Writing
4. Financial independence
5. Training people
6. Industry leadership
7. Creativity
8. Multiple streams of income

Jay's T-Bar in 1992

POTENTIAL JOBS	POTENTIAL INDUSTRIES
1. Writer	1. Sports
2. Trainer	2. Employment or job
3. Speaker or presenter	management
4. Marketing and	3. Motivation and empowerment
communications	4. Tourism
5. Manager	5. Business consulting
6. Adventure guide (tourism)	

Six to Eight Jobs and Industries That Provided Employment Opportunities for Me in 1992

1. Medical sales and healthcare positions—nurses, techs, and administrative jobs
2. Employment services including résumé writing and career coaching
3. Transportation—shipping, trucking, railroad, and planes
4. Distribution—warehouse management, shipping and receiving, traffic management
5. Import-export—sales, sourcing and purchasing, governmental and business liaisons
6. Personal health and fitness
7. High tech, computer, and Internet
8. Law enforcement and security—public and private

Notes, reflections, and breakthroughs: Through this process, I realized that I always enjoyed writing, speaking, marketing, and training. I also realized that if I had problems identifying and securing a rewarding job or career, many others out there must be in a similar situation. This presented a unique opportunity, and so I focused on employment services (item 2) from the list above.

The Four Global Options

There are only four global options you have when considering a new job or career. Write down the job you last held or are working at cur-

rently. Then write down the industry you last worked in or are currently working in.

Job:
Industry:

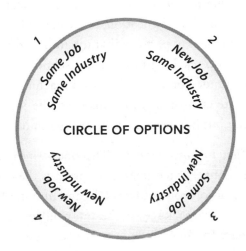

Now that you grasp the BIG picture, which includes your life values,
your career values, your T-Bar, and current market conditions, it's time
to consider the four global options. I call these *global* options because,
in reality, these are the only four job or career options you have.

■ *Option #1: Same job–same industry.* Choosing Option #1 means
you enjoy both the job and the industry you are currently in and, most
likely, need only conduct a job campaign to seek out a new company
or organization. For example, a fifth grade teacher who is teaching in
a public school may seek the same job (teacher) in the same industry
(public school system) but only needs to look at a new school in the
same school district or to apply for a teacher's position in a new school
district.

■ *Option #2: New job–same industry.* Option #2 means you enjoy
the industry but need to identify a new job within that industry. Using
the fifth grade teacher as an example again, she remains in education
but might seek a new job as an assistant principal or librarian. Or

perhaps if she wants to earn more income, she might consider becoming a sales professional selling to educational institutions. The job campaign will focus on education, but she will identify and pursue a new, more inspiring and rewarding job within that industry.

■ *Option #3: Same job–new industry*. If you select Option #3, it means you enjoy your job or vocation, but you need to identify a new industry or environment to perform that job in. The fifth grade teacher might consider a job teaching in a private school or learning center (new industry or venue), or she might seek a teaching or training position in a corporate environment. In this case, the job campaign will focus on teaching but in a new, more appealing industry or venue.

■ *Option #4: New job–new industry*. This option means you are ready for a wholesale change. Oftentimes this option is the option of choice if there's a career or job you've always dreamt about. Or possibly you have a nice severance package or the financial means to return to school and prepare for an entirely new career. Possibly the fifth grade teacher always had a passion for antiques. In this case, she might pursue a job as a manager or even an owner of an antique store. Perhaps she'll make the decision to stay home and be a full-time mom. The job campaign will focus on an entirely new job or activity in an entirely new industry or venue.

What Is Your Preference—Your Gut Instinct?

Take time and contemplate these four global options. Perhaps two of the options are appealing to you. In that case, write them down in the priority that is most exciting and appealing to you. In the case of the fifth grade teacher, maybe she selects Option #1 as her first choice and Option #2 as her second choice.

How I Came to Make My Decision

When I was fired in 1992, I held the job of marketing director for a company in the automotive aftermarket industry. I spent an entire weekend reviewing and evaluating my values, my T-Bar, the job market, and my four global options. It took me about four hours before

I selected Option #3, same job in a new industry. I discovered that I enjoyed marketing because it integrated many of my career values, including writing, creativity, and training. However, I was a fish out of water in the automotive industry. This was not the industry for me.

By taking quality time to consider my options, I had a major breakthrough! My heart was aching for a marketing job that would satisfy my career value of helping others. My brain went to work and came up with a life-changing idea. Why not use my talents and passions to market people? In other words, why not use my marketing skills to help people market themselves in competitive job markets? I could assist individuals to effectively identify, pursue, and secure jobs they wanted. I figured that companies and organizations hire professional marketers to package and position their products and services for competitive markets, so why wouldn't individuals hire a professional marketer to package and position them for competitive job markets? This idea felt right. For the first time in my life, I felt this is what I was meant to do! I was excited and became totally committed to this goal.

A Word About Bridging

Bridging is a term used to describe a multistep process of going from where you are to where you want to be. A doctor has to take multiple bridges before she can become a licensed physician. She has to travel on the undergraduate bridge for 4 years. Next she needs to cross the medical school bridge for another 4 years. Then there's the residency bridge, internship bridge, and possibly a fellowship bridge to cross. She has more than 10 years of "bridging" to do before she becomes a licensed physician!

I had to spend five years on the "get-to-learn-your-new-industry bridge," studying everything I could about career and job management. I attended as many training courses as I could and met as many industry leaders as possible. I also worked nearly three years writing my own book and helped create the first-ever professional résumé writing and career coaching association. But I also needed to make a living. So I had to cross the "résumé writing bridge" before I became a motivational career coach. I began writing résumés as marketing documents rather than as assembly-line, look-alike biographies, and soon I developed a national reputation. You see, the résumé writing bridge helped propel me into the career coaching profession and my own company. I have to admit, I met a lot of resistance along the way. Some family members insisted I was unrealistic. One close friend doubted I could actually make a living writing résumés while I prepared to become a motivational career coach. When I began writing my first book in 1994, one naysayer told me I had a better chance of getting to the moon than getting a book published!

The most important lesson I learned was that *anything was possible if I was committed to it.* This is a most valuable lesson for you as well. Anything is possible if you are committed to and passionate about your goal. I suggest that you must not give anyone permission to rob you of your dreams or let anything get in the way of attaining your true potential. Accept constructive advice but ignore negative voices.

I Don't Have the Money to Achieve My Dreams

When I was out of work in 1992, I had no money, no savings, and no idea what I wanted to do for a living. But I had studied too many people who went from poverty to millionaire and billionaire—including Oprah, Sylvester Stallone, JC Penney, Colonel (Harland) Sanders, Henry Ford, and Ray Kroc, the man who transformed McDonald's into an international household word—to give up on identifying and pursuing my dream. Now that I had an exciting goal to become a marketing coach for job seekers, I knew that my success depended less on what resources I had than how resourceful I could be. So this is an important principle for you to embrace as well. Know that it's never lack of resources that stands in your way of your ambitions; it's a lack of personal resourcefulness.

It didn't happen overnight. I worked long hours, met significant obstacles, and fell flat on my face more times than I care to remember. I found that rejection was a daily event that I had to learn to accept and deal with. On the other hand, I met some of the greatest people I've ever met in my life, and I helped many people secure jobs they otherwise would not have landed. And though it took longer than expected, by 1997 my dream of becoming a published author finally came true when McGraw-Hill offered me the first of what would be many book deals.

If I were to meet the friend who fired me back in 1992 today, I would thank him for that life-changing gift. Though I didn't know it then, he freed me to be able to identify and pursue my dreams. *Whatever you are experiencing at this time in your life, it is a gift in disguise, though it may not seem so at this moment.* Remember, you are guided by your values—about six to eight things that make you happy at any given time. Go back and make sure you have put 100 percent of your heart and soul into these assignments. Like a jigsaw puzzle, all the pieces are there. You just have to have the patience and discipline to put them together!

If the Answer Doesn't Come Today or Tomorrow

We didn't get to the moon in a week, a month, or a year. It took nearly 10 years to get there. And NASA experienced a number of setbacks and tragedies along the way. Just because the answers don't come today or tomorrow doesn't mean you stop pursuing them or quit on yourself and your family. Instant gratification is not a virtue; patience and persistence are. Be innovative, resourceful, and relentless in pursuit of identifying a job or career that will inspire an extraordinary life. You owe it to yourself and your family.

Profits May Be Better Than Wages

A monumental shift has taken place in the world economy and throughout the global job market. The industrial complex, predicated on manufacturing and production capabilities in the United States and in most industrialized nations, has been declining and will continue to decline or experience stagnant growth. When the Cold War ended in the early 1990s, approximately 2 billion people around the world were poised to enter the free market system, to make the shift from communism to capitalism.

Not surprisingly, outsourcing and global competition on a scale never seen before have emerged. Low-cost manufacturing is taking place, not just in China and India, but in Indonesia, Vietnam, and many of the former Soviet Union–dominated countries. Billions of people are beginning to climb the capitalist ladder that Americans and people in industrialized nations began climbing a century or more ago. Global competition will expand and intensify in the future; it's not going away.

And let's not forget that technology is also having a major impact on the job market. Technology and automation are replacing jobs. ATMs are replacing bank tellers; self-service checkout technologies are replacing cashiers; telecommunication technologies are replacing telephone operators, order takers, and a host of other customer service jobs—robots are replacing humans. So the two major factors contributing to the unprecedented shift in the job market are (1) the expansion of capitalism and free enterprise globally and (2) the technology revolution.

Not only is the job market changing, but the economic landscape for businesses and corporations is also changing. Even well-established and highly recognized companies are facing global competition and rapid technology integration and must fight just to survive. As a result, job security, jobs for life, company-paid health benefits, and many other security-based guarantees are gone forever. Businesses and organizations can no longer assume responsibility for the management and well-being of their employees. It is now the responsibility of individuals to assume control over their careers.

Unlimited Opportunities

The good news is that for the first time in history, we live in a world where there are virtually unlimited opportunities. Never before have you been able to reach out and touch 7 billion people on planet Earth... for free! By using social media, company websites, Skype, and other Internet and technology-driven tools, you can open new doors of opportunity around your community or around the globe. You can find job openings you couldn't find before. You can establish new contacts for jobs and income opportunities using social media sites like LinkedIn and Facebook. You can explore new markets anywhere in the world and access infinite information online.

That said, entrepreneurialism, full- or part-time, may be a viable option for many in the new transformational job market. When people consider the prospects of becoming entrepreneurs, many think of investing large sums of money in franchises or in start-up enterprises. Yet, a one-person electrician can operate his own entrepreneurial enterprise. An employee turned contractor can operate her own small business. Consider this: if you spend a few months trying to land a new job, what guarantees do you have that you won't wind up with the wrong boss, that a merger won't occur, that bankruptcy won't be filed, or that some other situation won't arise that will lead to you becoming unemployed and having to start another job campaign? How many times will you opt to invest a good amount of time campaigning for jobs that might not last long?

When you can no longer depend on companies and organizations for your family's financial well-being and security, you may have to take matters into your own hands. This is not the place to discuss the intricacies and strategies of starting and operating a business enterprise. But this is a good time to get you to start thinking about the possibilities of doing so. As the economy and job market adjust to the new realities of global competition, machines replacing people and even world events that affect day-to-day work, you may want to consider entrepreneurial opportunities. Whether you work at your own business full- or part-time, become an independent contractor, purchase an existing business, start up your own venture, open a home-based Internet or network marketing business, or partner with others, entrepreneurialism (self-reliance) may be the best hope for providing a steady income for you and your family. Yes, there are risks to this option. So the entrepreneurial alternative must be studied and researched very carefully. But if job security is anywhere on your list of values, you just might discover that the best chance you have of satisfying that value is to put your future in your own hands, not those of an employer.

Finally, if you do opt for traditional jobs, become an entrepreneurial employee. This means taking responsibility for consistently delivering more in value to your employer than you are compensated for.

This means investing in your own professional development and skill attainment to ensure your value to your employer is always expanding. Entrepreneurial employees show up early, stay late, and always do more than what's expected. They bring a positive and motivated attitude to the job every day and treat their job as their own business.

Multiple Jobs and Income Sources

From my early teens through college, I always worked at multiple jobs. I had two paper routes, mowed lawns, shoveled snow, worked construction, labored in a leather factory, was a store detective, worked summers as a camp counselor, pumped gas (before technology eliminated that job), and sold greeting cards, just to name a few! I always had multiple income sources. Even if I was terminated from a job, it never affected me because I always had plenty of other ways to earn money.

Then, when I completed college, I bought into the idea that I should put all my eggs in one basket. In other words, once I graduated from college, I allowed myself and my family to be at the mercy of one employer. I purchased a home and took out a mortgage. I purchased an automobile and took out a car loan. I suddenly began to live in fear because, for the first time in my life, I had placed my financial security and well-being in the hands of one source, one company, one boss. Does this make any sense to you? I was told how many sick days and vacation days I was entitled to. I was told what insurance plan I qualified for. I was told how to dress. I was sent to training seminars on how to speak and act the way the company wanted me to speak and act. I was told when I had to work late, over weekends, and during my vacation—whether I liked it or not, all this in the name of so-called job security and a weekly paycheck.

I never experienced financial stress prior to graduating from college because I had multiple income sources. After I completed college, I experienced nothing but financial stress. However, at age 26, I reverted to my successful model of multiple income sources. I figured I could watch TV and make others rich, or I could spend evenings working on different ways to earn extra money and make myself rich! I chose earning money and ensuring my own security over watching television and other non-income-producing activities.

How about you? Are you ready to change your thinking and take control over your financial future? You might opt to weave multiple part-time jobs together rather than rely on one employer. Perhaps you'll choose to supplement a full-time job with a part-time position or a part-time business venture. The main message here is that security must be redefined as "taking care of yourself rather than putting your life and the welfare of your family in the hands of others." Being an entrepreneur and creating multiple streams of income can be exciting and highly rewarding options if you plan properly and go about it strategically.

In any case, it is important that you recognize that the U.S. as well as the world economy and job market are going through an unprecedented time in human history. The world has always been in a state of change, but today, with the onslaught of technological advances, what used to take 60 years to change now changes in about 60 days! Indeed, the price of gasoline alone changes every few minutes! Human beings, for the most part, are creatures of habit and feel best operating in their comfort zone. They don't particularly embrace change. And yet today, those who will survive and thrive in the new economy will be those who embrace, prepare for, and adapt quickly to change.

You may have to head back to the classroom on a regular basis to attain new skills and knowledge so you don't become inconsequential to the marketplace in the future. You may have to work nights and weekends at multiple jobs to maintain the quality of life you aspire to. You may need to consider moving and relocating more often to venues (national and international) that offer more lucrative employment opportunities. All this is neither good nor bad; it is what it is. But let me remind you that today anything is possible. You live in a time where extraordinary opportunities are available to creative, hard-working individuals who embrace change. Master the strategies in this chapter because in the transformational economy and job market we live in, you will need to reinvent yourself and your career over and over again. When you know your values, have inspiring goals, are prepared for constant change, and are ready to work hard because you know it's the best investment you can make in your future, you will begin the liberating process of creating employment opportunities that you enjoy and that inspire your whole life!

STEP 2 SUMMARY

- You must first acknowledge that the purpose of your job or career is to empower your life so you can achieve all that you want to achieve in life. Ask the two most important life questions in order to live a full and rewarding life: (1) "What do you want to get out of life?" and (2) "What do you want to give back to life?"
- The starting place for helping you identify your next job or career opportunity is not by determining what kind of job you want to work at, but rather by determining what kind of life you envision for yourself.
- You must determine your signature values because this is the only way you can be happy, live a fulfilling life, and work at a meaningful job. Values, unlike beliefs, come from the heart, not the head. When you identify your signature values, you will do very little thinking. You will allow your heart to feel what makes you happy.
- To determine your life and career values, ask the question, "What's most important to me in my life or career that will make me happy and that will significantly enrich the quality of my life?" Identify your top eight values and prioritize them in the order of importance that naturally makes you happy.
- Once you have established your life and career values, grade them individually according to how happy you are living in harmony with them. By doing so, you will have a clear understanding of what you have to work on to live a full and rewarding life and what you have to work on to identify a full and rewarding job.
- Control what you can control. Evaluate your grades and then revise them wherever possible. This will help raise your level of

happiness so that you can better address the more pressing issues. Understand that your life's values will constantly shift and change. You must be prepared to review and revisit your values and hierarchy on a regular basis.

- When you explore new job and career options, you need only define (1) jobs that would interest you, that you are qualified or wish to do, and that are in harmony with your career and life values and (2) industries that interest you. Use the T-Bar model to brainstorm jobs and industries that you would enjoy. When you have completed working the T-Bar brainstorming exercise, place your list in a hierarchy where the most exciting jobs and industries are atop the list.

- Study the job market where you live or where you are seeking work. You must know what jobs and industries are on the rise and what ones are on the decline. Once you have performed an in-depth study of your market, write down the top six to eight jobs and industries that currently provide the best opportunities.

- Put all the pieces to the career puzzle together in one place. This way, you'll have the information readily available so you can see the BIG picture in order to make BIG decisions.

- Use the Circle of Options model to determine if you want to work in the same job–same industry, new job–same industry, same job–new industry, or new job–new industry. These are the only four global options you have.

- Use the technique of bridging to go from where you are to where you want to be. This is used when you determine that it will require multiple steps to get there.

- Don't ever quit on your dreams or settle for less than you can be. If you don't come up with the answers the first time around, go back and redo the assignments in this chapter. Just because the answers don't come today doesn't mean they won't come tomorrow or sometime next week. But one thing is for certain. If you do quit on your dreams, they will never have a chance!

- Consider entrepreneurialism—this might be a full-time or part-time venture, or it could be a one-person business or a larger enterprise. Profits may be better than wages. At a time where there is little job security, the best job security may be that which you provide for yourself.

- To protect yourself, your family, and your financial future, consider multiple income sources. It may not be the best strategy to put all your eggs in one basket or depend on one employer.

3

USING VALUE-BASED RÉSUMÉS AND SELF-MARKETING TOOLS

Average Résumés and Online Profiles Won't Attract the Jobs You Want at the Pay You Deserve

The Value-Based Résumé

Let me make this as simple as I can. *Your résumé must STAND OUT and communicate your value to prospective employers!* No successful product or service is marketed with the intention of blending in with its competition. Why would you? In the United States alone, at any given time, there are at least 40 million people looking for jobs. There are job seekers who are unemployed, underemployed, unhappily employed, and happily employed seeking to become even more happily employed. You have competition! So your résumé must be unique and professionally present you in a manner that differentiates you from other qualified job candidates who are seeking the same jobs you want.

In competitive job markets, look-alike, assembly-line résumés won't get the attention of hiring authorities. Hiring authorities, including human resource professionals, executive recruiters, and hiring managers, don't have time to read stacks of boring biographies from strangers. They want to know quickly what specific contributions you can make and results you can produce.

> By definition, a value-based résumé is a self-marketing document that communicates your ability to produce significant results better than other qualified candidates.

You have 100 percent control over what you include in your résumé and how you present your self-marketing document. Unfortunately, most job seekers don't take advantage of their power. When you effectively and strategically control the information on your résumé, you will elicit attention and enthusiasm from prospective employers and win interviews and job offers. Unquestionably, most résumés being circulated today are nothing more than what I call *chronological obituaries*—uninteresting documents prepared on white paper with black ink and formatted like 40 million others. Not only do they all look alike; they also don't communicate enough to differentiate the applicant from other competing candidates. Most résumés don't address prospective employers' needs, problems, or organizational objectives. They don't shout out why the person is the best candidate for the job. In a global, highly competitive job market, there are way too many competing résumés in circulation for you to submit a blend-in-with-everyone-else résumé. Your résumé must STAND OUT if you have any chance of attracting outstanding job opportunities quickly. Your résumé must be reader-friendly yet powerful in its messages. Your résumé must be exciting and professional, and it must be a document that you are proud of and that will effectively promote and sell you to prospective employers.

A value-based résumé offers a number of specific advantages such as the following:

1. *Market value.* The process of creating a value-based résumé will result in your being able to effectively identify and communicate your value to prospective employers. Your résumé will clearly communicate bottom-line results and organizational contributions you can produce

and deliver that position you as a highly qualified and valuable candidate.

2. *Differential factors.* When you strategically develop your value-based résumé, you will want to identify differential factors that represent highly valuable skills, qualifications, and other labor assets that set you apart from your competition. Differential factors often tip the hiring scale in your favor! For instance, if you have an industrywide reputation, your reputation might be a differential factor. If you are a black belt in Six Sigma, that may constitute a differential factor. A number of years ago, I coached a chief financial officer who worked for a legendary golf professional. Having worked for a famous golf professional was a differential factor because many hiring managers found it intriguing to interview (and hire) someone who worked for a celebrity. Perhaps you are bilingual; this may represent a differential factor. When you identify factors that differentiate and distinguish you from other qualified job candidates, you'll provide your job campaign with a distinct advantage in landing a job quickly.

3. *Confidence builder.* When you design and create a value-based résumé that communicates your value and those attributes that set you apart from your competition, and present it in a fresh and exciting format, you gain a whole new level of confidence in yourself, your ability to promote yourself, and your ability to remain self-motivated throughout the entire job campaign. You will be proud of what you are marketing—namely, you! You will approach each day with a renewed sense of self-worth, knowing that you truly STAND OUT from others, and this advantage will result in rapid employment.

4. *Door opener.* Value-based résumés open the right doors. Exciting, well-presented, value-based résumés open doors of opportunity that otherwise would not open for you. Your résumé will race to the top of the pile because it bellows out to employers, "This is what I can do for you—why I am a good fit for your company and the best candidate for the job."

5. *Stronger, more effective interviewee.* Value-based résumés lead to interviews, and interviews lead to job offers. When you write your résumé strategically thinking about the interview, you begin developing the key messages you'll eventually want to communicate in an interview to win the job. In other words, when you take the time to properly prepare your résumé thinking about the key value messages that will win job offers, you'll then showcase those messages on your résumé to win interviews!

Rules for Writing Value-Based Résumés

There are no rules! The goal of your résumé is to STAND OUT from your competition and to get prospective employers excited about the prospects of interviewing and hiring you because of the value you bring to their organization. Rules mean conformity. How can you STAND OUT or distinguish yourself from other job seekers if you blend in with them? Coca-Cola doesn't package itself to look like Pepsi. AT&T doesn't package itself to look like Verizon. Ford doesn't package itself to look like Chevrolet. And you shouldn't package or present yourself to blend in with your competition.

Of course, there are a number of guidelines I might suggest, the critical one being to promote your value. This is why I call these résumés *value-based* résumés. I've listed 12 guidelines for you to consider for today's job market. But in the end, you have to think hard about what strategy will work most effectively for you. Then, execute it.

■ *Guideline #1: Make your case in 15 to 20 seconds or less.* Most hiring authorities claim they spend 15 to 20 seconds, at most, reviewing your résumé to determine if they want to read more of your document and invite you in for an interview. In that 15- to 20-second window of opportunity, you must communicate your value, showcasing and headlining those qualities that ring out, "I'm a highly qualified candidate worthy of a closer look!"

■ *Guideline #2: Keep the résumé as brief as possible.* Today, given the myriad of voices vying for attention and the scores of résumés that are crossing the desks of hiring authorities, shorter is better. A solid one- or two-page résumé is the norm, but not without exception. If you have a strategic reason to write a résumé longer than one or two pages, by all means do so. Some employers expect longer résumés if candidates have an extensive list of published material, projects, or speaking engagements. And many federal résumés require three, four, or more pages of information. But be careful not to conduct the interview in the résumé or ask the reader to labor through pages and pages of "stuff." Be precise and on message, and keep your résumé as brief as possible.

■ *Guideline #3: Remember for whom you are writing the résumé.* In most cases, you're writing your résumé for a stranger who doesn't know you at all. Your main objective is to understand what prospective employers are looking for and then to provide that information clearly on your résumé. Do prospective employers want to read your biography, or do they prefer to know how you can contribute to their organizational goals? Before you write your résumé, seek first to understand the needs of potential employers, and then communicate, on your résumé, how you can best meet those needs.

■ *Guideline #4: Résumés without achievements are like report cards without grades.* Hiring authorities and prospective employers know that a key indicator of future performance is past performance. It's not what you did in the past that determines your "hirability"; it's how you performed—the results, achievements, and contributions you delivered in the past that matter most. Your résumé is not the place to be humble! It's the place to professionally and confidently showcase your past achievements and to blow your own horn—loud and clear!

■ *Guideline #5: Select your vocabulary with meticulous care.* Did you increase sales or orchestrate explosive growth in revenues? Did you provide good levels of customer service or deliver unparalleled levels of quality customer service? As a receptionist, did you merely greet people, or were you the manager of first impressions? Are you a good problem solver, or can you resolve complex issues professionally and expeditiously? Words are power, and keywords and phrases are powerful agents for eliciting the right emotions to enthusiastically engage prospective employers to want to read your document and interview you. Well-chosen words can be the difference between an interview and job offer and a missed opportunity, so select your words and messages with careful precision.

■ *Guideline #6: Be sure the résumé is well organized and reader-friendly.* It won't help much if you have extraordinary skills and qualifications but a hiring manager is unable to access the information. Take care not to use many different fonts or bullets. Balance your information with white space so the document is pleasant and easy to read. Consider limiting the use of italics, as information presented in italics is normally difficult to read. The presentation should be crisp, exciting, and inviting. Yes, when you look at your résumé, you want to be proud of it. But remember that you are writing the document for prospective employers and want the document to be easy and pleasant to read so they get excited about you!

■ *Guideline #7: Be professionally innovative and different.* Yes, you can use pictures, graphics, and graphs on your résumé, *if it is appropriate and strategically sound to do so.* Yes, you can use color, shading, and boxes so messages JUMP OFF THE PAGE! Yes, you can include short references or testimonials within the résumé itself. That being said, you must know your audience and play to their emotions and expectations. Some forums still require a more traditional presentation. Be as bold and innovative as you can without coming across as gimmicky or foolish. Be confidently courageous and professionally astute.

■ *Guideline #8: Test-market your résumé.* When you have completed writing your résumé, identify five to seven people whose opinions you value and ask for their honest feedback. You may want to show it to a human resource manager, an executive recruiter, or an English teacher. Ask these five to seven people if you left anything important out or if there is something that needs to be deleted. Have them look for any lingering typos, grammatical errors, or format inconsistencies. When you have five to seven sets of eyes review your résumé, chances are you'll end up with a perfectly constructed document that you can be proud of and that will open the door to your next job!

■ *Guideline #9: Address potential problems on the résumé.* Indeed, this breaks with traditional "rules." The employment landscape has changed over the past few decades where many companies have gone out of business or have reduced their labor force. As a result, possibly you've worked at many jobs in a short time frame where you might be perceived by a prospective employer as a job-hopper. In this case, you might want to list "reasons for leaving" for all or some of your former jobs. Or maybe you had to take time off to care for a family member and have an employment gap. In this case you might want to communicate this on the résumé. Do not ignore these challenges; rather, address them on your résumé. If you're not sure how to effectively do this, seek advice. If potential red flags appear on your résumé and you don't address them, chances are you won't get asked in for an interview.

■ *Guideline #10: Don't confuse your audience.* The résumé must flow well. You want to build excitement and positive momentum while prospective employers read through your document. You don't want hiring authorities to suddenly stop reading your résumé because they are confused. You don't want to lose the attention of your readers by confounding them with overlapping jobs, dates that are out of order or inaccurate, conflicting job titles, or a disorganized format. Your résumé should be easy to read, easy to follow, and easy for readers to understand.

■ *Guideline #11: Embellish at your own risk.* Employers are well aware that many job seekers will embellish, exaggerate, or outright lie on their résumés to secure employment. This is nothing new. However, keep in mind that today employers are conducting extensive background and reference checks more than ever before. If you are untruthful on your résumé in order to get your foot in the door, chances are when they find out, you'll get the boot.

■ *Guideline #12: Hire a professional.* Most people are uncomfortable selling themselves. They lack objectivity, are reluctant to boast about themselves, and haven't been taught how to skillfully and confidently market themselves to a competitive job market. They find it difficult to know what employers want to read on résumés and how best to present themselves in all facets of the job campaign. The process of planning and conducting an effective job campaign can be complex and, oftentimes, overwhelming. And this is where coaches, trainers, and mentors can be invaluable. Isn't it true that most successful companies hire advertising agencies and marketing firms to help promote their products and services? Don't athletes and celebrities have agents that promote them? Don't politicians have a campaign manager and a staff of people to advise them? Whom do you have working for you? You, most likely, are not an expert at marketing yourself. On the contrary, you've been conditioned, if not instructed, to be humble and unpretentious. So if you are unable to create a résumé or any self-promotional tool that powerfully positions you to outcompete your competition, you may want to seriously consider hiring a reputable professional who can.

The Four Questions That Value-Based Résumés Must Answer

Your résumé must answer four critical questions, and the first three questions must be answered in 15 to 20 seconds. The four questions are:

1. What position(s) are you seeking or what are you qualified to do that would be of value to our company or organization?
2. What results and contributions can you make better than other qualified candidates?
3. What skills, qualifications, and strengths do you bring to the job that would lead us to believe you can produce the results you say you can produce?
4. Can you provide specific results (achievements) that you produced in the past that would indicate that you can produce them in the future?

The Law of Messaging

The *law of messaging* states that for most jobs, there are about six to eight messages that you have to communicate that will make 90 percent of the difference between getting an interview and not getting an interview and between getting a job offer and being a runner-up. Said differently, there are only about six to eight things that determine 90 percent of your value to prospective employers. Consider, if you will, the U.S. presidential election process. There are only a handful of issues (about six to eight) that candidates run on to win the job of U.S. president. Whichever candidate makes the best case in addressing those few issues wins. The same holds true for most jobs. When you identify those six to eight messages that are most important to prospective employers and will make the biggest difference in getting interviews and job offers, you'll design your résumé (and your job campaign) around those messages. This alone gives you a significant advantage over your competition. The messages must collectively answer the questions, "Why should I hire you?" and "What makes you the best qualified candidate for the job?"

There are three types of messages that will be used to create the showcase or headline you will place at the top of your résumé. It is in the showcase section of the résumé where you will communicate your powerful 15- to 20-second value message indicating that you are a highly qualified job candidate! The three types of message are:

1. The *Ultimate Results* messages
2. The *Core Strengths* messages
3. The *Differential* messages

1. The Ultimate Results Messages

The Ultimate Results messages are the most important messages you can communicate because they are the most essential messages prospective employers want to see on your résumé. Again, it's all about what you can do for them! The Ultimate Results messages communicate to prospective companies and hiring authorities your value, your worth to them—in other words, what you get paid to produce.

An effective way to determine the Ultimate Results messages is to answer the following questions: *If you were to be hired today, what specific performance standards will you be measured on at your first annual review—a year from now?* You get paid for producing results, so *what results will you produce that will indicate to a company that you are worth hiring?* When you answer these questions, you will have identified your Ultimate Results messages. What follows are examples of the Ultimate Results messages for five different jobs (I will use the same five jobs to illustrate all three messages).

A Teacher

- To significantly enhance the educational experience leading to an enriched and rewarding life for all students

A Sales Professional

- To significantly increase sales, expand market share, and provide unparalleled levels of customer service to contribute to organizational growth and profit objectives

An IT College Graduate

- To advance the goals and objectives of the IT department by utilizing strong programming skills and to improve organizational efficiencies and productivity through the use of state-of-the-art technologies

A Return-to-Work Candidate

- To utilize skills and abilities to meet organizational goals in a loyal, dependable, and professional manner

A CEO

- To increase global presence, product mix, and market share to improve and maintain shareholder earnings and value

When you correctly identify the Ultimate Results messages, you have identified the main reason a company or organization would hire and pay you. Not only will this STAND OUT on your résumé, but it will also make you a more confident and effective interviewee.

2. The Core Strengths Messages

Once you have identified your Ultimate Results messages, you have only to determine your six to eight core strengths that would lead hiring managers or prospective employers to believe you can produce the Ultimate Results. *Core strengths would include skills, qualifications, and talents you have that make you valuable and that are the most important job requirements as perceived by prospective employers.* The Core Strengths messages are messages that communicate those specific skills and qualifications that you will use in your day-to-day activities to produce results and meet or exceed company performance standards.

An effective method for identifying these qualities is to pretend you are writing a book entitled *The Six to Eight Skills You Must Master and Qualifications You Must Have to Become an EXTRAORDI-NARY* [insert your particular job title, profession, or vocation here]. What would those six to eight skills and qualifications be? Imagine you'll write an entire chapter for each skill and qualification to ensure readers of your book that they are mastering the right skills and attaining the right knowledge and qualifications to be EXTRAORDINARY at their jobs.

Be careful not to be too general or overly fluffy when identifying your Core Strengths messages. It's fine for graduating students or return-to-work candidates to say they have good organizational and communication skills, are loyal and dependable, are "people" persons, and are results oriented. However, these would not be valuable messages for a senior executive because they are too general for this job level. Core Strengths messages for senior-level executives might include being highly skilled in mergers and acquisitions, identifying and capitalizing on new and untapped market opportunities, turning around underperforming operations, and utilizing knowledge gained in an MBA program to develop best practices to optimize efficiency and ensure strong bottom-line performance.

The following are eight Core Strengths messages for each of the five sample professions I noted previously. They follow the Ultimate Results messages.

A Teacher
- To significantly enhance the educational experience leading to an enriched and rewarding life for all students
  1. Improve reading and writing skills
  2. Establish classroom management and discipline

3. Integrate real-life experiences into the classroom
4. Introduce real-life experiences outside the classroom
5. Serve as an effective student-parent liaison
6. Work collaboratively with administration and peers
7. Possess strong academic credentials
8. Have nine years of experience supported by excellent references

A Sales Professional

■ To significantly increase sales, expand market share, and provide unparalleled levels of customer service to contribute to organizational growth and profit objectives
   1. Perform in-depth market analysis and create growth plans
   2. Generate leads and engage in strong networking activities
   3. Demonstrate high-impact presentation and closing skills
   4. Assess client needs and effectively overcome objections to sale
   5. Establish new territories and turn around underperforming ones
   6. Initiate new product or service launch
   7. Identify and capitalize on new and existing business opportunities
   8. Provide groundbreaking levels of customer service

An IT College Graduate

■ To advance the goals and objectives of the IT department by utilizing strong programming skills and to improve organizational efficiencies and productivity through the use of state-of-the-art technologies
   1. Perl, MySQL, Linux, Apache, Mason, XML, XSL, HTML, JavaScript, Java, MS C11, ASP, 8086 Assembly, Fortran, COBOL, network firewall and hackproof server installation and configuration, and automatic mass website building
   2. Internet-based public relations for online applications
   3. Network administration
   4. Wireless applications
   5. Speech recognition
   6. Excellent customer service skills

7. Complex, technical troubleshooting and problem-solving abilities

8. Projects delivered on time and within budget

A Return-to-Work Candidate

■ To utilize skills and abilities to meet organizational goals in a loyal, dependable, and professional manner

1. Excellent phone skills
2. Good communication skills
3. Sound judgment, good decision-making skills
4. Good character: honest, trustworthy, dependable
5. Assignments completed on time
6. Willingness to go the extra mile
7. Team player
8. High school graduate

A CEO

■ To increase global presence, product mix, and market share to improve and maintain shareholder earnings and value

1. Mergers and acquisitions
2. Reengineering and change management
3. International corporate leadership experience
4. Visionary strategist; identify and pursue new growth opportunities
5. Board member and shareholder relations management
6. Developer of world-class teams to achieve world-class results
7. MBA from the University of Michigan in international business
8. Skilled in raising capital for growth and expansion

3. The Differential Messages

Differential messages communicate added value that you bring to the job that goes beyond the call of duty or that simply distinguishes you from the competition. In other words, Differential messages communicate to potential hiring managers and prospective employers not only that you have the skills and qualifications to do the job better than other qualified candidates, but that *you bring more to the job than what's required.* Differential messages, which may be one skill or qualification or a number of them, can be the difference between a job offer and a rejection letter. In many cases, Differential messages are the critical messages that separate you from job seekers with similar skills, abilities, and education as you have. I often refer to them as *tip-the-scale-in-your-favor factors.*

For example, suppose you are seeking a job as a retail manager. The Differential factor might be that you are fluent in English, Spanish, and French. Being trilingual may not be part of the job description but can be a valuable asset when working with diverse employees and customers who speak Spanish and French. Possibly you are seeking a job as a fifth grade teacher. If you are highly proficient with technology and computer programming, these skills may not be part of the job description but might be perceived as having high value to an academic institution. If you are an expert electrician, but you are also skilled in sales, this added value of contributing to new business development might be the differentiator that will help you land a job quickly and at top pay.

When you combine the Differential messages with the Ultimate Results and Core Strengths messages, you will have all the self-marketing messages you need to create a powerful showcase for your résumé.

A Teacher
- *Differential message.* Have a master's degree in library science *(Able to assist and contribute to library and media services)*

A Sales Professional
- *Differential message.* Have an existing book of business *(Able to deliver immediate sales and growth opportunities)*

An IT College Graduate
- *Differential message.* Have a Dale Carnegie Public Speaking Certification *(Able to professionally train and present new technologies and services effectively to employees and customers)*

A Return-to-Work Candidate
- *Differential message.* Have own transportation and able to work a flexible work schedule *(Provides a great degree of dependabil-*

ity and flexibility compared with others who may be dependent on the bus or others unable to work a flexible work schedule)

A CEO

■ *Differential message.* Have built and managed two billion-dollar companies *(Able to build a third one)*

Once you have identified your Ultimate Results, Core Strengths, and Differential messages, you have a solid foundation upon which you can design the showcase of your résumé. You will have the key messages that will engage the reader and create excitement in 15 to 20 seconds.

Later, when you work on the employment and education sections, along with the other sections of your résumé, you will know exactly what job responsibilities and achievements and what educational highlights and internship experiences to emphasize that will provide clear and concise evidence that you can use your skills and qualifications competently to produce significant results!

The Showcase Format

The showcase format is a résumé presentation that communicates your Ultimate Results, Core Strengths, and Differential messages in 15 to 20 seconds professionally and in a reader-friendly manner. The showcase engages the reader and builds initial excitement in you as a viable job candidate. Pick up any newspaper or magazine and study the advertisements. In most cases, you'll notice a headline or see a picture with an accompanying headline. Effective marketing strategically positions information and pictures to capture the prospective buyer's attention quickly and with strong emotion. When you create your résumé, you'll also want to insert a headline atop the document to capture prospective employers' attention quickly and with strong emotion. It's your first, most important, impression!

When you review the sample résumés on the following pages, you'll notice that the three messages, the Ultimate Results, Core Strengths, and Differential messages, make up most of the showcase. Remember that your résumé must answer three questions in 15 to 20 seconds: (1) What position(s) are you seeking or what are you qualified to do that would be of value to our company or organization? (2) What results and contributions make you better than other qualified candidates? and (3) What skills, qualifications, and strengths do you bring to the job that would lead us to believe you can produce the results you say you can produce? Your showcase is designed to answer those three questions in that time frame. What follows are examples of showcases for a teacher and a sales professional.

Showcase for a Teacher

STEPHANIE SANDS

6868 SW Flagler Circle • West Palm Beach, FL 33401

(561) 555-8787 • e-mail@e-mail.com

Seeking position as . . .

Teacher/Educator

Combining Outstanding Technology, Leadership, and Teaching Experience

Master's Degree in Library Science

Strong desire to enhance the educational experience for all students, leading to enriched and rewarding lives

Personal Introduction

A seasoned professional with a passion for combining technology experience and educational qualifications to make a significant contribution in the field of education.

Core Professional Strengths

- Energetic presentation/teaching skills
- Maintain classroom discipline
- Work well with culturally diverse populations
- Meet individual/group needs
- Extracurricular participation
- Facilitate established curriculum
- IT/technology
- Real-life integration
- Problem solving/conflict resolution
- Effective student-parent liaison
- Work well with superiors and peers
- Professional/highly ethical

Showcase for a Sales Professional

HECTOR GONZALEZ

21009 North Shore Avenue • Winnetka, IL 60093

(847) 555-9119 • e-mail@e-mail.com

SENIOR-LEVEL SALES & BUSINESS DEVELOPMENT EXECUTIVE

Significantly Increase Sales/Expand Market Share

Outmaneuver Major Competitors to Establish Market Dominance

- 25 years of success in ever-changing global economies
- Lead generation, networking, and relationship building
- Perform in-depth market analysis; create strategic/ growth plans
- Identify and capitalize on new and existing marketing opportunities
- Territorial start-up, turnaround, and growth management
- Build and nurture key strategic alliances and partnerships
- Key account management/retention; ensure unparalleled levels of service

Have existing book of business to increase sales immediately

Senior-Level Sales Executive with a reputation for providing unparalleled levels of customer service and contributing to organizational growth and profit objectives.

The Two Components
of the Employment Section

Once you have developed a compelling showcase, you are ready to answer the fourth question that your résumé must address: Can you provide specific results (achievements) that you produced in the past that would indicate that you can produce them in the future? In most cases, the employment section will answer this final question. However, if you are a graduating student or one who has little or no direct work experience, your internships, academic highlights, and extracurricular activities, including volunteer work and community service, will be emphasized.

When you work on the employment section, you'll want to address two distinct components for each job or position that will appear on the résumé: (1) your detailed job responsibilities or job description and (2) your achievements and contributions, the results you produced. How you accomplish this is up to you. What follows are two samples of how most hiring professionals, human resource managers, and executive recruiters expect the employment section to appear.

Preferred Presentation
(Job Description PLUS Bulleted Achievements)

GREAT SCOTT UNIFORM COMPANY, Boston, MA 20xx to Current
General Sales & Operations Manager

Directed the successful start-up of a niche-market law enforcement uniform company specializing in private security and in-house security organizations. Company generates $3.6 million in annual revenues serving clients nationwide. Divide time equally between sales and operations. Presently supervise 19 employees including warehouse manager, alterations manager, sales coordinator, and office manager. Fully responsible for a 9,000 sq. ft. location including a 6,000 sq. ft. warehouse with $350k in inventory. Coordinate proactive safety and security protocols. Establish key benchmarks to optimize efficiency and productivity. Develop/manage a $1.7 million annual operating budget, coordinate purchasing and vendor relations, and ensure high customer service standards for more than 190 national accounts. Full charge P&L responsibility.

Specific Accomplishments
- Grew start-up operation to an industry leader generating $3.6 million in annual sales.
- Developed company "brand label" (*Great Scott*) that improved market share 18%.
- Private labeling efforts increased sales 47% and boosted gross profit margins 11%.
- Achieved 16% net profits—some 7% above national industry average.
- Spearheaded Just-In-Time inventory process that reduced inventory 21%.
- Identified 3 profitable acquisitions that added $600,000 in yearly sales.
- Closed 4 national accounts boosting annual sales $1.1 million.
- Awarded "Distributor of the Year" by *Made to Measure Magazine.*
- Awarded "Quality Dealer" award by *Made to Measure Magazine* 7 consecutive years.
- Positioned company for successful/profitable sale, with 1-year working contract.

Next Best Presentation
(Job Description and Achievements
Combined in a Bulleted Format)

GREAT SCOTT UNIFORM CO., Boston, MA   20xx to Current
General Sales & Operations Manager

- Directed the successful start-up of a niche-market law enforcement uniform company.
- Manage $3.6 million operation with a $1.7 million annual budget.
- Divide time equally between sales and operations. Presently supervise 19 employees.
- Manage a 9,000 sq. ft. location including a 6,000 sq. ft. warehouse ($350k in inventory).
- Grew start-up operation to an industry leader generating $3.6 million in annual sales.
- Developed company "brand label" (*Great Scott*) that improved market share 18%.
- Private labeling efforts increased sales 47% and boosted gross profit margins 11%.
- Achieved 16% net profits—some 7% above national industry average.
- Spearheaded Just-In-Time inventory process that reduced inventory 21%.
- Identified 3 profitable acquisitions that added $600,000 in yearly sales.
- Closed 4 national accounts boosting annual sales $1.1 million
- Awarded "Distributor of the Year" by *Made to Measure Magazine.*
- Awarded "Quality Dealer" award by *Made to Measure Magazine* 7 consecutive years.
- Positioned company for successful/profitable sale, with 1-year working contract.

Personal Information

Unless there is a strategic reason to include it, I suggest you leave off personal information including age, place of birth, marital status, and other such information. Remember, though, there are no rules. If you have a legitimate reason for including personal information, do so. For instance, when you prepare a federal résumé for federal jobs, you may be asked to supply federal job compliance information including your social security number, proof of citizenship, gender, and date of birth. Once again, think strategically. *Put yourself in the place of a hiring manager who will be reading your résumé,* and ask yourself, "If I did not know this person (meaning you), would the personal information be at all relevant or important to the hiring process?" If so, put it in. If not, leave it off.

Religious and Political Issues

The same general guidelines apply for religious and political information as they do for personal information. I advise you to leave all information relating to religious, political, and other possibly controversial activities and subjects off the résumé unless you have a strategic reason to include it.

Salary and Salary History on Résumés

As a rule, salary history is not included on résumés. If you are seeking a federal job, you may need to include prior pay grades and salaries on your document. And if a job posting requires that you provide salary requirements or history, you'll want to provide that information. But *the general guideline is that unless you have a tactical reason for doing so, omit salary from your résumé.*

Reasons for Leaving Prior Employment

Traditionalists will argue that you never include reasons for leaving on your résumé. However, times have changed. If you have had many jobs in a short period of time, which might cause you to be perceived as an unreliable job candidate, you will want to provide short, effective, and nondefensive reasons for leaving prior positions. If you had to leave a job to care for an ill parent, this might also be a time when you would include a reason for leaving. The important thing to remember is that you want to include reasons for leaving if they enhance your ability to better communicate with hiring authorities for the purpose of neutralizing or eliminating influences that could be perceived as negative. *Caution:* There is a fine line between providing understandable reasons for leaving and coming across as overly defensive. The reasons must be well thought out, brief, and strategically sound.

Gimmicks and Omissions

What is a gimmick to one person may be a foot in the door to another. Marketing and self-promotion are about capturing the emotions of a prospect; they're about attracting attention and communicating that you are qualified to fill an employment vacancy. I have successfully used pictures, graphs, color, cartoons, testimonials, graphics, and other nontraditional strategies to help thousands of people land great jobs at great pay, at all levels! Years ago a well-respected executive recruiter from New York suggested that if candidates are going to err, they should err on the side of originality and creativity, not boredom and the same old, same old. She told me that at least the creative résumés will get noticed; the boring ones won't see the light of day. So here's the best advice I can offer. Create a professionally exciting document! I would argue that gimmicks don't work. But creativity and a refreshing presentation supported by rich content (your value) offered in a professional manner will STAND OUT and get read.

One last important point I must make here. People who read résumés and hire employees are not stupid. It doesn't make sense to include dates in your employment section but leave them off in your education section because you don't want to show your age—they'll determine your age from the employment section dates. They know all the tricks! Be tactical in your approach, don't underestimate the intelligence of hiring and employment professionals, and beware of the consequences of coming across in a scheming, deceptive, or unprofessional manner.

Education and Training Experience

If you have a bachelor's or master's degree, you do not have to include your high school education. Include the highest degrees you have, but use common sense; you don't have to go back to middle school. In addition to formal education, employers want to know what you do to continually expand your knowledge and improve your professional skills. Indeed, change takes place at lightning speed these days, and employers want to know that you are keeping up with the speed of change. One senior hiring manager once told me, "I don't ever want to hire anyone who goes to bed as ignorant as he woke up!" What this manager meant was that it's important that you commit to constant and never-ending professional improvement. That said, what continuing education courses have you attended? How many personal development seminars have you completed? How many professional improvement workshops have you attended in person, online, or by audiobooks or videos? What computer skills are you proficient in that are relevant in today's job market? This important information should be included on your résumé in addition to your formal education. Additionally, unless you have strategic reasons to place them elsewhere, your education section is a good venue to include all pertinent licenses and certifications and any other credentialing you might have earned that is relevant to your next job.

Where you place the education section within the résumé is up to you. If your education is about the same as that of your competition, it probably should appear after the employment section. On the other hand, if your education can be positioned on your résumé as a unique "selling point" and may be more impressive than that of most of your competition, you might want to put the education section before the experience section. If you are a recent graduate, you may also want to position the education section before the experience section. Internships can go in the education section or in the employment section, or they can have a section of their own. Remember, this is an exercise in self-marketing, and you must strategically control how you want the reader to read the résumé.

Military Experience

If you have military experience, first, thank you for your service. Three hundred million-plus Americans are indebted to you. So I urge you to present your military information on your résumé as proudly as you wore the uniform. However, include only relevant information that would interest prospective employers. For instance, if you served 25 years ago, you need only list the branch of the service you were in, title, rank, possibly where you served, honorable discharge, and dates of service. If you spent the past three years in the armed services maintaining and repairing vehicles and are seeking a civilian job repairing automobiles, you will treat your military section the same as you would the employment section, noting both your specific responsibilities and your key achievements, awards, and contributions. Include only information that is directly or indirectly relevant to your next job.

One last important thought: be sure you translate military verbiage into business verbiage. For instance, rather than stating that you reported directly to your CO, write that you reported directly to your supervisor. Many civilian hiring managers are not familiar with military language or acronyms, so it is your responsibility to present a résumé in a language they will understand.

Relevant Activities and Professional Affiliations

If you have space on your résumé and want to include relevant activities and professional affiliations, include them. If you are a member of professional associations, trade organizations, and business groups, include them. If you have volunteered or are active in community service projects, include them. If you play golf and, in your line of work, deals are consummated on the golf course, include this. On the other hand, if you are seeking a position as a bookkeeper and you like to travel and enjoy gardening, unless you are looking to become a traveling bookkeeper or are trying to land a bookkeeping job with a landscaping company, it might be best if you leave this off the résumé.

Use common sense and include only information that hiring authorities will find valuable in making a favorable hiring decision.

Don't Conduct the Interview in the Résumé

Here's a good analogy. Your résumé is like a book report. You don't tell the whole story in a book report; you simply provide a synopsis of the key highlights that STAND OUT as the most important information taken from the book. The same is true when writing a résumé. Your résumé must dangle the carrot, but not tell the whole story. Your résumé must communicate your value and enthusiastically engage the reader, not provide a long-winded, never-ending biography of your professional life. Your résumé must provide highlights of your professional experience that prospective employers would find valuable. Do not tell the whole story; don't conduct the interview in the résumé.

Cover Letters

Most people today, including hiring authorities, are living a high-stress, information-overload life. They are bombarded by e-mails, voice mails, U.S. mail, and junk mail. They take calls from cell phones, business phones, and home phones and send and receive text messages, not to mention the demands for attention they get from many other voices including their bosses! *Most HR managers, executive recruiters, and hiring managers are placing less and less importance on cover letters.* Yes, they are still a part of the process, but in most cases, they play a less significant role. The reason for this is simple: in the short-attention-span world that we live in today, they just don't have the time to read them. If your résumé is strong and effective, the cover letter becomes a very short, formal introduction to your résumé. That said, if you have a valid reason for writing a long cover letter or are asked to submit a comprehensive letter of introduction, you must do so with great care. But generally speaking, your résumé must do the talking and promoting. Here are eight tips for writing effective cover letters:

1. Address the cover letter to a specific person, making sure you have the correct name, title, company, and address. This shows respect for the person you are sending the résumé to.

2. "To Whom It May Concern" salutations should be used only if you can't determine the name of the hiring person or the company (for instance, when responding to a blind ad).

3. If you were referred by someone, be sure this is included in the first sentence of the cover letter: "Jennifer Wells suggested I contact you in regard to an accounts receivable position you have open..." It's an attention grabber.

4. If asked to include salary history or requirements, you must address this or risk being disqualified. Provide a range, such as, "Over the past five years I have earned between $35,000 and $48,000. However, I am open to any reasonable offer consistent with my ability to produce results and meet your performance expectations." If asked for salary requirements, use the same strategy: "I am aware that the salary range for a loss prevention manager in the Houston area averages between $75,000 and $110,000. Given my experience and, most importantly, my ability to make significant contributions to your company, I would hope to be on the upper end of this scale."

5. If you are sending the résumé out electronically, the cover letter can be inserted as the e-mail itself; just attach your résumé. If you prefer that your cover letter is the first page of the attachment, that's fine. But the general guideline is not to attach multiple files. Make it easy on the hiring manager and send only one attachment or file to open.

6. Do not rehash what is on the résumé. This is disrespectful of the reader's time. If you have done a good job with your résumé, you want the cover letter to quickly invite the hiring manager to review your résumé.

7. Cover letters should not be preachy. Sales managers know that sales are the heartbeat of any company; you don't have to lecture them on this. Nurse supervisors know the importance of compassionate patient care; you don't have to tell them what they already know. Keep the letter short and concise. The cover letter is not the place to preach or teach. It's the place to entice recipients to read your résumé!

8. Finally, the four most important words on the cover letter are "*I respect your time*." The following cover letter is a sample template. Notice the first four words of the second paragraph.

ROBERT SMITH

200 Main Street • Hollywood, FL 33021

(954) 555-2345 • e-mail@e-mail.com

May 24, 20xx

Mrs. Patrice Wellington, Assistant Manager

Beachwear International

3232 Ocean Boulevard, Suite 300

North Miami Beach, FL 33089

Dear Mrs. Wellington:

Diane Smith suggested I contact you as I am interested in applying for the position with Beachwear International as Purchasing Manager. I have enclosed my résumé for your review and am certain that I can be a valuable asset to your team and meet the goals and objectives for this position.

I respect your time and feel confident that my value, past achievements, and ability to contribute are well outlined in my résumé. If you feel, as I do, that I would be a significant member of your professional staff, I would welcome an interview at your earliest convenience.

Thank you for your consideration, and I look forward to hearing back from you.

Sincerely,

Robert Smith

Encl.: Résumé

A Case for Multiple Résumés

If you have multiple job objectives, you may need multiple résumés for each objective. The competition for jobs today is intense. Many job seekers are creating individual résumés for each job they are applying for, knowing that to get an interview it is critical that each résumé communicate precise messages that are aligned with the specific job requirements. The skills sets, qualifications, and value messages are different for a sales associate than a sales manager, just as those skills are different for a manager seeking an executive-level position than a mid-level position. In fact, the skills sets, qualifications, and value messages may be different for a teacher seeking a position in a public school than a private school. And if you are considering a job as either a social worker or a customer service representative, you'll need two completely different résumés because the skills sets, qualifications, and value messages are completely different. Landing a job rapidly requires an innovative and dedicated effort to distinguish yourself from the competition you're facing and to connect favorably with prospective employers. This means you'll probably need to develop multiple versions of your résumé to precisely align your skills and qualifications with the specific requirements of each job for which you are applying. Sometimes the changes and modifications are subtle; other times they will be more pronounced. When it comes to landing the right job at the right pay quickly, don't be lazy! Create multiple résumés, because your competition probably won't. Undoubtedly, this gives you a BIG advantage!

The Reference Portfolio— the Secret Weapon to Rapid Employment

The reference portfolio is a powerful tool that deviates from traditional ways of thinking about job search, but it is a tried and true strategy for successful sales and marketing campaigns—including the job campaign! The truth is, the reference portfolio may be the most effective tool you'll have in your job campaign arsenal. But before we go any further, stop and grab a few books from your library shelves. Look on the back covers of the books. Chances are, you'll see a number of testimonials, most of which are only two or three sentences in length. But each testimonial sings the praise of the book and entices potential readers to want to purchase and read the book. A reference portfolio works the exact same way! A reference portfolio is a one-page document with four to six testimonials that will sing your praises and entice hiring professionals to want to meet and hire you!

I have already noted that hiring managers, headhunters, employment recruiters, human resource professionals, and most people who hire employees view most résumés with a healthy concern and a good degree of skepticism. They pretty much assume, be it true or not, that most job candidates embellish, exaggerate, and outright lie on their résumés. A reference portfolio is a powerful and influential tool to eliminate the negative manner in which most hiring professionals will read your résumé! The portfolio is made up of professional references that will confirm and validate that the achievements and contributions you noted on your résumé are truthful and accurate. If you are a student or a recent college graduate, are returning to the workforce after a prolonged absence, or have limited professional references, you'll want to identify those references, professional and personal, who will attest to the fact that you are a valuable and viable candidate able to produce results and contribute to organizational goals.

Once you have identified and confirmed that four to six people agree to endorse you, I advise you to write the reference statements yourself! Athletes and celebrities do not write the advertisements for the products and services they endorse. And your "endorsers" probably should not write the advertisements for you, either! I suggest you write the testimonial and then send it to your references so they can review the statement and make whatever changes they may want to make. Once the reference is complete, they should keep a copy in their files so when a prospective employer calls them to validate their reference about you, they can easily refer to it. This may not be entirely comfortable for you, and that's okay. Allow yourself to be a little uncomfortable, because when you write the references, *you control time and content*. If you leave it to your references to write them, they'll procrastinate as long as they can. And the truth is, most want you to write them anyway. So by writing them yourself, you save precious time. Also, if you want your references to write about your specific achievements and contributions but, instead, they write that you're a nice person who works hard, you undersell yourself. Remember, this is a proactive job campaign! Take the initiative and manage what you can control—like time and content. This is consistent with achieving rapid employment.

Once you have it completed, I suggest the reference portfolio be the final page of the résumé. If you have a one-page résumé, the reference portfolio will be page two. If you have a two-page résumé, the reference portfolio will be page three. One of the many advantages to having a reference portfolio is that you don't need to have numerous reference letters on company letterhead. Besides, most companies are unwilling to provide them. If you have a boss who will give you a reference but can't do it on company letterhead or on company time, he or she may be willing to do so via a personal e-mail address from home.

Finally, once you have a reference portfolio, you can add the following postscript (P.S.) and insert it at the bottom of your cover letter, or e-mail if you are sending your résumé by e-mail. **And I suggest you bold it so the P.S. is a focal point of the cover letter or e-mail.** By doing this, the hiring professionals reading your résumé will do so, not with healthy skepticism, but with confidence that what they are reading is, indeed, accurate and truthful.

> **P.S.: I have included my reference portfolio to assure you that the information and achievements contained on my résumé are truthful and accurate.**

A Sample Reference Portfolio

JUSTIN T. WINTERS

1750 Greystone Court • Lansing, MI 48912

(754) 555.3232 • Cell: (754) 555.1212

e-mail@e-mail.com

REFERENCE PORTFOLIO

John P. Hendricks, Director of Operations   e-mail@e-mail.com
THE MIDWEST GOLF COMPANIES

"Justin Winters was the best assistant warehouse manager The MGC has ever had. He single-handedly designed and implemented a JIT inventory program that reduced inventory 23% while improving customer services levels to a record 98.7%. He is well respected by the 13 employees who report to him, and he always motivates highly productive teams."

Ed Shuman, Senior Buyer   (212.555.6012)
PING CORPORATION

"Justin Winters is the ultimate warehouse management professional. As assistant manager for The Midwest Golf Companies, we worked exclusively with him and developed a positive and effective win-win relationship. He negotiated a number of innovative terms and conditions with our company that reduced his organization's on-hand inventory levels 25% but increased annual sales volume with our company 15%. Justin's innovative program was so successful, we are now offering it to our customers nationwide. He is creative, resourceful, and relentless in meeting his company's growth and bottom-line objectives; and firm but fair in his relations with vendors."

Susan B. Johnston, Assistant Warehouse Manager   (561.555.7279)
SOUTH MICHIGAN GOLF OUTLET

"I would not have the job I have today without the training, supervision, and inspiration of Justin Winters. I worked for Justin when I worked for Midwest Golf for 6 years. During that time, he taught me how to be a highly effective leader in warehouse management. So few people ever get the opportunity to learn from a true professional and an authentic human being. I can't imagine anyone more qualified than Justin to be a warehouse manager in a high-volume, growth-driven environment."

Frank Fordum, Warehouse Manager   **e-mail@e-mail.com**
THE MIDWEST GOLF COMPANIES

"Justin Winters has worked as my assistant warehouse manager for the past 9 years. There is not one aspect of high-volume warehouse operations that he is not proficient at. In fact, it is said that everyone is replaceable—but when Justin left our company, it left a void I am not sure can be filled, not only because of his extraordinary skills, but also because of the intangible attributes he brings to the job—like a smile on his face and a positive attitude every day. He is sorely missed."

Five Sample Résumés

Five sample résumés follow. Please pay particular attention to how the showcases for each discipline include the Ultimate Results, Core Strengths, and Differential messages discussed earlier in this chapter and are nicely integrated at the top of each résumé.

These samples are provided so you can get an idea of how you can create your own exciting, value-based résumé. In this book, the résumés are printed in black and white, but you can use colored dividers and color print if appropriate. *The goal is to combine sizzle with substance!* When you clearly communicate your value in an exciting and professional manner, when you STAND OUT from the millions of boring, assembly-line, *chronological obituaries* that hiring managers dread going through, you'll begin to open doors of opportunity and land the job you want at the pay you deserve—quickly!

STEPHANIE SANDS

6868 SW Flagler Circle • West Palm Beach, FL 33401

(561) 555-8787 • e-mail@e-mail.com

Teacher/Educator

9 Years Outstanding Experience

Master's Degree in Library Science

**"Enhance the educational experience for all
students, leading to enriched lives"**

Introduction

A seasoned professional with a passion for education and making a significant contribution in the field. Recognized for collaborative approach in meeting quality standards, accomplishing organizational missions, and achieving positive change.

Core Professional Strengths

- Improve reading and writing skills; classroom management/discipline
- Integrate real-life experiences into and outside the classroom
- Introduce effective computer/IT technologies to enhance the learning experience
- Act as an effective student-parent liaison; work collaboratively with administration and peers

Formal Education

Master's in Library Science, 20xx

Florida Atlantic University, Boca Raton, FL

Bachelor's in Education, 20xx

University of Miami, Coral Gables, FL

- Board Certified, American Board for Certification of Teacher Excellence

Professional Experience

Palm Beach County School District, 20xx to 20xx

West Palm Beach, FL

Lower School Teacher

Responsible for all aspects of education at the lower school level with emphasis on math, English, science, social studies, and history. Ensure a positive learning classroom environment and work collaboratively with administration, peers, students, and parents to meet a broad range of objectives.

- Disney World Teacher Award (top 100 out of 5,000 teachers)
- Teacher of the Year finalist
- Recipient of Teacher of Excellence award
- More than 30 performance awards over past 7 years
- Nominated for WPEC News 12 Educator of Excellence award
- Delegate to National Teachers Convention, Washington, DC, 20xx to current
- Assisted more than 40 students in gaining admission to the prestigious School of the Arts

Experience Prior to 20xx

Middle School Teacher   Jupiter Elementary, Jupiter, FL
Lower School Teacher   The Baker School, North Palm Beach, FL

Relevant Activities

National Teachers Educational Association
Florida Society for Academic Excellence
Music Teacher/Assist in the Library Services

HECTOR GONZALEZ

21009 North Shore Avenue • Winnetka, IL 60093

(847) 555-9119 • LinkedIn: Hector Gonzales • e-mail@e-mail.com

SENIOR-LEVEL SALES & BUSINESS DEVELOPMENT EXECUTIVE

Significantly Increase Sales/Expand Market Share

Outmaneuver Major Competitors to Establish Market Dominance

- 25 years of success in ever-changing global economies
- Perform in-depth market analysis and create strategic/ growth plans
- Identify and capitalize on new and existing marketing opportunities
- Territorial start-up, turnaround, and growth management; product launch
- Build and nurture key strategic alliances and partnerships
- Key account management/retention; ensure unparalleled levels of service

Have existing book of business to increase sales immediately

Senior-Level Sales Executive with a reputation for providing unparalleled levels of customer service and contributing to organizational growth and profit objectives.

Professional Experience

CORPORATE PACKAGING, INC., Hollywood, FL   20xx to 20xx

Senior Sales Executive

Directed all B2B sales and new business development activities in the South Florida market servicing more than 180 major accounts generating $6.8 million annually. Performed market analysis and strategies to meet organizational sales and profit objectives. Assisted manufacturing and distribution clients in selecting proper packaging products to meet diverse needs. Helped clients with product specifications to produce customized packaging products.

- Grew new territory with $0 in revenues to $6.8 million.

- Closed key accounts including Ryder, Carnival Cruise Lines, and the Miami Dolphins.
- Prepared specs and won $8 million bid (over 10 years) with the City of Miami Beach.
- Worked with corporate development team to design new packaging equipment that is now generating more than $50 million a year in revenue nationally for the company.

OFFICE DEPOT, Deerfield Beach, FL   **19xx to 20xx**
Senior Sales Executive

Managed Broward County sales efforts selling upscale, high-end office equipment with an average ticket price of $6,500 to local businesses. Developed qualified leads, made comprehensive presentations to senior management, and closed key accounts in competitive market. Ensured high-quality service, making certain that products were delivered on time and properly installed. Trained clients in equipment usage.

- Grew new territory from $2.3 million in sales to more than $7 million in less than 4 years.
- Closed key accounts including hotels, hospitals, municipalities, and local businesses.
- Exceeded sales quota and revenue projections each year.

Military

UNITED STATES ARMY
Commander, Honorable Discharge, 20xx

Education

THE OHIO STATE UNIVERSITY, Columbus, OH
Bachelor of Science: Civil Engineering, 20xx

Skills and Credentials

- Computer Skills: Word, Excel, PowerPoint, Outlook, Social Media Marketing, and Internet Applications
- Certified Social Networking Professional, Suarez Institute of Social Networking

RYAN ROBINSON

9844 Colonia Way • S. Hackensack, NJ 07605

(201) 555-7337 • e-mail@e-mail.com

Entry-Level IT Professional with Strong Academic/ Work Experience

Quick learner and performer, with strong working knowledge of software, hardware, networking, programming, operating systems, and security applications

A highly creative, technically skilled individual seeking to advance the goals and objectives of the IT department by utilizing strong programming skills. Poised to improve organizational efficiencies and productivity through the use of state-of-the-art technologies.

Core Strengths:
- Ability to diagnose, troubleshoot, and resolve technical problems.
- Exemplary academic record. Graduated with 3.52 GPA.
- Outstanding communication skills (verbal/written); excellent customer service skills.
- Project management—conception through completion including budget/expense control.

Operating Systems: Windows and Mac

Applications: MS Office (Word, Excel, PowerPoint, Access, Outlook, Publisher), Norton Utilities, Adobe Photoshop; Perl, MySQL, Linux, Apache, Mason, XML, XSL, HTML, JavaScript, Java, MS C++, ASP, 8086 Assembly, Fortran, COBOL, network firewall and hackproof server installation/configuration, and automatic mass website building; Internet-based public relations for online businesses; network administration (LAN/WAN, TCP/IP, VPN) and wireless and voice.

Valued-Added Contributions: New business development; social media optimization

Education:

Bachelor of Science: Computer Science   20xx

University of Arizona, Tucson, AZ

• Vice President, University of Arizona IT Club

• Honors Graduate; Member, Pi Beta Alpha Honor Society

Internships:

Allan Research International, Tucson, AZ   **Summer 20xx, 20xx, and 20xx**

Tech Support Intern: Operated as service point-of-contact for help desk, helping to diagnose, troubleshoot, and resolve up to 11 tickets a day. Assisted in converting from Windows to Mac for 38 workstations. Provided daily technical support for e-mail, network, connectivity, telecommunications, peripheral equipment, and system maintenance. Set up computers and installed software. Helped transfer help desk requests from e-mail to web-based system, reducing IT response time by 21%.

Part-Time Work in College:

University of Arizona, Tucson, AZ   **20xx, 20xx, 20xx, and 20xx**

Help Desk Technician: Tutored students in various operating systems and software applications. Served as mentor in computer labs and provided emergency technical support for early-morning shift. Helped install 19 new Macs and 13 PCs for high-volume lab.

Keywords: Entry-Level, Systems Administrator, Network Administrator, Technical Help Desk Coordinator, Technician, Systems Support Engineer, Systems Analyst, PC Technician, IT Troubleshooter, Team Player, Project Management, MAC and PC Expertise, Client Relations, Voice Recognition, Programming, Social Media.

TARA JOHNSTON

123 Main Street • Atlanta, GA 30339

(555) 363-1234

Seeking HOUSEKEEPING POSITION with Hotel or Hospital

Bilingual: English and Spanish

A loyal, trustworthy, and dependable individual with own transportation and able to work a flexible work schedule. A lifelong record of hard work, going the extra mile, and producing excellent results. A good working knowledge of the equipment, materials, and methods used in cleaning and housekeeping work.

Strengths

- Organized and goal oriented
- Take the initiative to solve problems
- Interpersonal skills; a people person
- Perform tasks well on short notice
- Follow instructions and company policies
- Complete multiple assignments on time
- Able to make good decisions
- Team player and work well with others

Activities 19xx to Current

Over the past 20 years, I have successfully raised four children; one has graduated high school, and the other three are in middle and high school. I have always been self-supporting, performing housecleaning chores on a regular basis. I always managed my schedule to meet my customers' needs while being a responsible mother.

Over the past 20 years, I have worked for about 15 customers. Basic responsibilities include cleaning homes and following specific instructions for each customer. I have a detailed list for each customer to be sure all work that needs to be completed is completed to my customer's satisfaction. I pride myself on going the extra mile at all times.

I have never lost a customer (except when they moved or passed away). I make recommendations to customers when repairs around the home are needed. I provide weekly lists for all customers for specific supplies and equipment I need to do my job. I am trustworthy, loyal, dependable, and bondable.

Education/Activities

Pooley High School, Atlanta, GA

High School Graduate

- I am an active member of the PTA.
- I sing in the church choir.
- I volunteer weekends at a homeless shelter.

References

Mr. and Mrs. Wilson DeVos (Customer, 11 years)	(555) 987-6543
Mrs. Wilma Jefferson (Customer, 11 years)	(555) 345-6789
Mr. and Mrs. David Goldfarb (Customer, 14 years)	(555) 456-2348
Mr. and Mrs. John Crow (Customer, 8 years)	(555) 912-8348

HAROLD R. CONNORS

7177 Beacon Circle • Boston, MA 01977

(617) 555-3232 • LinkedIn: Harold Connors

e-mail@e-mail.com

"C" LEVEL OPERATIONS/MANAGEMENT EXECUTIVE

MBA, University of Michigan

Increasing Shareholder Value in Publicly Traded and Private Companies

SEC Reporting & Compliance/Start-up and Turnaround Management

Technology Integration/Business Development and Market Expansion

P&L Responsibility/Cash Flow Management

Executive Profile

Senior Executive with a reputation for accelerated revenue growth, operational and strategic improvements, and bold visionary initiatives. High-profile career with a solid track record for consistently enhancing growth, profits, and shareholder value.

Areas of Expertise

- Mergers and acquisitions
- Reengineering and change management
- Board member and shareholder relations
- Raising capital for growth and expansion
- International corporate leadership
- Recruit and develop world-class teams

Professional Experience

DRUCKER ENTERPRISES, Waltham, MA   20xx to Current
CEO

Recruited by Board of Directors to direct and grow this leading biotechnology, orthopedic, reconstructive implants, trauma, sports medicine, and general medical instruments company. Divide time equally between new business development, operational productivity, corporate finance, regulatory compliance, and product line expansion.

- Sales: $174 million
- Market Share: 17%
- Employees: 168
- Management: 18 (including 5 VPs)
- Locations: Main headquarters and 9 satellite locations throughout the U.S.
- Stock Value: $19 (17% annual increase on average over the past 5 years)

Past 5 Years' Highlights

- Recruited VP of Sales and expanded U.S. market share 19%; infiltrated Caribbean market the past 2 years
- Recruited VP of Finance and increased annual earnings and shareholder value 17% on average a year
- Recruited VP of HR to attract top talent, enhance corporate training, and optimize productivity
- Expanded product line and developed proprietary products resulting in $25 million a year in additional sales
- Expanded from a single location to 9 satellite offices including Chicago, LA, Dallas, and Orlando
- Recognized in *New England Journal of Medicine* as the Top Medical Instrument Company in our market

KENNEDY MEDICAL, INC., Detroit, MI   20xx to 20xx
Executive Vice President

Kennedy Medical is a distributor of orthopedic products with sales of $23+ million. Recruited to turn around an unprofitable operation due to lagging sales, customer service deficiencies, and operational inefficiencies. Performed in-depth operational and market analysis and created a 5-year growth plan with the goal of tripling sales and reducing operating expenses by 20%.

- Tripled annual sales in 5 years from $7.5 to $23 million while increasing net profits 13% a year
- Identified a new market segment including orthopedic surgeons, neurosurgeons, and maxillofacial surgeons
- Reduced fixed overhead 11% a year and implemented an incentive-based program to reduce variable costs

- Created a comprehensive quality assurance program resulting in 98.7% customer retention rate
- Oversaw total knee replacement patient outcome and survivorship clinical studies for a highly respected medical research organization. High exposure led to significant new business ($6 million+)

Education

UNIVERSITY OF MICHIGAN, Ann Arbor, MI

- MBA (International Business), 20xx
- Bachelor of Arts Degree (Economics), 19xx

Affiliations

- American Business Association
- National Orthopedic Reconstructive Implant Society
- American Orthotic & Prosthetic Association
- American Prosthodontics Society
- The Association for Children's Prosthetic Orthotic Clinics
- American Orthopedics Society for Sports Medicine

References and Supporting Documentation Furnished upon Request

A Word About Bios

Bios are normally one-page documents providing key "essentials" that represent one's value to a targeted audience. They are used primarily by independent contractors, business owners, entrepreneurs, and those who do not feel résumés are appropriate for their purposes. Bios might appear on a website, in a brochure, in a business plan, or as part of a consulting proposal.

The following is a sample bio. Though the sample bio is lengthy, some bios are much shorter. Many people create a comprehensive bio that can then be edited and shortened to meet varying needs.

Talbot K. Sutter

3955 Success Boulevard • Palm Beach Gardens, FL 33410

(561) 555-1234 • e-mail@e-mail.com

LinkedIn@LinkedIn.com

PRESIDENT/REAL ESTATE BROKER
Sutter & Nugent, Inc.

Luxury Real Estate Specialist
South Florida/Florida

Talbot K. Sutter is a lifelong resident of Palm Beach Gardens, a third-generation Palm Beach County, Florida, native. Talbot is a graduate of The Benjamin School (North Palm Beach) and holds dual bachelor's degrees from Florida State University in Real Estate and Finance.

Upon graduating from Florida State University, Talbot moved back to his home town in Palm Beach Gardens and began his real estate career. He was fully committed to a career in real estate before he graduated Florida State, securing his Florida real estate license well before he completed his education. Talbot immediately jumped into the industry with Illustrated Properties, a well-respected company that had been a dominant force in the industry for over 35 years. In his two years with the company, Talbot was appointed Director of a new division responsible for technological enhancements and improvements. He recognized that the real estate industry, like most other industries, was in a technology-driven transition and understood that technology integration, in combination with traditional sales and marketing strategies, would best serve his customers. As a result, Talbot was awarded "Top Producer" in 2012 and 2013.

Talbot possesses a work ethic that is second to none. He provides unparalleled levels of service to his customers because (1) he is completely committed to helping them achieve their goals and expectations, (2) he understands the market and offers advice and information that is invaluable to his customers, and (3) he is a market visionary—he sees emerging trends to best position his customers to take full advantage of them. But Talbot's rapid success is a result of attributes that extend far beyond his extensive real estate knowledge and expertise, and they are his two most important values: *integrity* and *professionalism*.

In January 2014, Talbot formed Sutter & Nugent Real Estate, a full-service upscale residential and commercial real estate company, to better serve his customers and to provide a level of personal service rarely found in the industry. The company specializes in working with sellers and buyers in the Palm Beaches and throughout Florida, with emphasis on luxury properties, waterfront real estate, and premier neighborhoods.

Talbot says that "when you work with a real estate company, goals and expectations must be achieved. But just as important are the experiences and relationships we create in pursuit of the goals and expectations. That's what makes Sutter & Nugent unique: we want you to enjoy the experience as well as the outcome."

Case Study Portfolios

The last communications tool is the case study portfolio. In the past, case study portfolios were developed primarily for senior-level management executives and professionals seeking positions at $150,000 and up. However, today case study portfolios are being used by anyone seeking a clear advantage in landing the best job opportunities. A case study portfolio is an employment tool that can best be described as a mini interview. Recall the law of messaging mentioned earlier in this chapter. You now know that about six to eight messages make 90 percent of the difference between getting an interview and not getting an interview, between getting a job offer and getting a rejection letter. When you identify those key six to eight performance messages, you will then come up with six to eight of the most impressive situations (case studies) that you encountered that would unquestionably demonstrate your professional competencies.

Challenge, Strategy, and Results

For each case study, you'll want to describe (1) the challenge you faced, (2) the specific strategies you used to successfully address the challenge, and (3) the results you achieved as a result of implementing the successful strategies. A good length is a half page per case study, or two case studies per page. Developing a strong case study portfolio is important for a number of reasons: (1) It forces you to go back into your past work history and identify your greatest accomplishments, achievements, and contributions. Most people tend to take themselves and their victories in life and in their jobs for granted. (2) You will be much better prepared for your interviews because you will have specific cases or situations you can talk about that will indicate to the interviewer that you can achieve significant results. (3) This is an innovative and notable tool to include with your résumé or as a "leave-behind" following an interview. Using a case study portfolio is yet another way to differentiate yourself from other qualified candidates seeking to win the job you want. For sure, 99.9 percent of your competition won't have one!

When to Use a Case Study Portfolio

If you are seeking a position at a yearly compensation level of $100,000 and above, you may want to consider including your cover letter, résumé, reference portfolio, and case study portfolio in one volume (hard copy or one electronic file). If you are pursuing a position that pays less than $100,000, you may want to consider including your cover letter, résumé, and reference portfolio, but save your case study portfolio for the interview. It may be overkill to submit a case study portfolio for positions paying less than $100,000. I reiterate one more time that there are no rules. You are conducting a job campaign, not a job search, and must assume personal responsibility for your own campaign. You must make strategic decisions and take the right constructive action that works best for you so you land the job you want quickly.

What follows are four sample case studies; each case study depicts a different profession or job. Study these samples and then be creative and mindful in developing your own portfolio.

Case Study for a Forklift Driver/Supervisor

The Challenge: Disorganization

I recognized that there were serious problems in the warehouse where restocking and order-picking activities interfered with each other. Neither activity was performed at optimal efficiency, not to mention the numerous forklift collisions, downtime and associated costs, and worker's compensation cases.

The Strategy

I scheduled a meeting with the warehouse, shipping and receiving, and customer fulfillment managers. I described the chaotic, unproductive, and unsafe nature of operations. The warehouse looked like the Indianapolis Speedway, with forklifts racing to fill the bins with incoming inventory competing for aisle space with forklifts racing to fill customer orders. I suggested a new logistical traffic system that would result in an effective and safe environment. The warehouse floor was redesigned and color-coded to better control traffic flow and reduce, and actually eliminate, accidents while improving efficiency and productivity.

The Results

Customer orders were filled 38 percent quicker, and the receiving and stocking of new merchandise improved 25 percent. Forklift accidents virtually ceased, saving the company over $600,000 a year (forklift repairs and worker's compensation claims).

Case Study for a Retail Manager

The Challenge: High Employee Turnover

I came to the realization that our high employee turnover was having a severe negative impact on sales and customer service at our prestigious fashion boutique on Worth Avenue in Palm Beach. Customers expected personalized attention from seasoned and established sales associates. Clients continually complained about the high turnover of employees and the inexperience and unprofessional nature of new associates.

The Strategy

Corporate policy limited pay increases, so I developed a proposal for corporate to allow a 40 percent discount on all clothing purchased by our sales associates for themselves AND for immediate members of their families. (Previously employees were entitled to a 15 percent discount for themselves only.) I also suggested that all sales associates receive a $250 bonus every six months they remained with the company—a loyalty gesture. I provided clear evidence that these changes not only would pay for themselves but would significantly increase sales and customer loyalty and retention.

The Results

A pilot program was implemented, and within six months, employee turnover was reduced from 90 percent to less than 10 percent, customer satisfaction skyrocketed, and sales increased 20 percemt. The program was so successful, it was adopted nationally.

Case Study for a Secretary

The Challenge: Outdated Phone System/Poor Service

Customers were becoming irate. The phone system was so antiquated, customers were being left on hold too long, and calls were being inadvertently disconnected; tension throughout the office was reaching the boiling point. Management, however, was not overly enthusiastic about investing $60,000 in a new phone system.

The Strategy

With the President's authorization, I went on Craigslist and eBay and began researching preowned phone systems, seeking out a viable system that would improve the company's efficiency and customer service and sales while saving the company tens of thousands of dollars.

The Results

I located an Avaya Partner Telephone System for 15 lines and 40 phones or 12 lines and 32 phones—complete with all the state-of-the-art "bells and whistles." The exact same system retailed new for $59,000 (including full installation). I negotiated a price of $9,800 and then located a local company that would install the entire system for $3,000. Coming with a five-year warranty, this fully refurbished system saved the company $46,200 and played a significant role in improving efficiency, sales, customer relations, and employee satisfaction.

Case Study for a Chief Information Officer

The Challenge: Sales Processes Were Antiquated and Unproductive

The company had 15+ sales professionals serving more than 3,000 accounts throughout New England. Customer orders would come in to the Order Department via e-mails, faxes, text messages, voice-mail messages, handwritten messages, and carrier pigeons. Many customer orders were lost, filled improperly, delayed, and mishandled. Statistics indicated that approximately 20 percent of all orders experienced minor-to-major errors or problems. Customer satisfaction was at an all-time low (below 80 percent), and overall sales were stagnant from the previous year.

The Strategy

I performed extensive industry research and identified a software program (OrderRite) that integrated and aligned with our current order processing software and would work well on iPads. The company made the investment and issued iPads to all sales professionals with OrderRite software installed. All sales professionals attended a training session on the system and were informed that all orders, without exception, had to be placed on their iPads as soon as the orders were taken. This was the only way orders would be accepted by the Order Department.

The Results

Productivity was greatly improved. Orders came in immediately with no delays. Sales personnel spent 75 percent less time taking and processing orders, and order fulfillment accuracy increased from 80 percent to 98 percent. Customer satisfaction improved from a low of 79 percent to over 90 percent, and sales over the previous year increased by more than 15 percent in the first three months alone. The Order Department was more productive, and overtime was reduced almost 100 percent because of greater efficiencies and quality fulfillment activities.

Online and Social Media Tools

Rob Thomson, managing partner of Waterfront Properties and Club Communities in Jupiter, Florida, which is the largest purveyor of luxury real estate in the Palm Beaches, says:

> Whether you are seeking a job, more clients, or in some way, looking to achieve more in today's workplace, you must manage and optimize your online presence, your brand. You must have a highly professional LinkedIn profile. You must have a professional and strategically created Facebook page with appropriate posts, pictures, and content where prospective employers and customers get to know, like, and trust you. I suggest you conduct your social life somewhere else, and use Facebook, LinkedIn, Google+, and all other online venues to land the job you want and advance your career. To me, it all comes down to one question: Do you want to use your social media and online sites to help your career or BS with friends? If you want to land a job quickly and make a fortune in the workplace, the answer seems very obvious to me.

Few can argue that today's world revolves around the Internet; we live in a world where most people depend on their smartphones, tablets, and computers to communicate and interact with one another. Texting has become more popular than phone calls or e-mails, and social media is changing the world—as well as how people land jobs! In this day and age, you can hardly go anywhere without seeing just about everyone glued to a phone or tablet. So it comes as no surprise that social media, or social networking, has had and will continue to have a significant impact on employment practices and hiring strategies.

Many job seekers are finding out about new job opportunities through social media. The vast majority of jobs are attained through networking and word of mouth, not by applying to online job postings. So strategic interaction using social media, particularly LinkedIn and Facebook, allows job seekers to learn about job openings they otherwise would never know about.

Recruiters and employment agencies use LinkedIn, a professional social media site, to find and recruit new employees. In general, between

75 and 90 percent of all headhunters use LinkedIn to search for candidates when filling job openings. In addition, more than 60 percent of hiring managers determine whether a job seeker's personality and values are a good match for their company just by viewing that job seeker's social media presence. Not surprisingly, somewhere between 80 and 95 percent of all employers search job candidates' names using search engines to see what shows up on the Internet before they make a job offer. Unfortunately, many job candidates lose job opportunities they otherwise would have landed because of negative pictures on Facebook, inappropriate postings, and an unprofessional, immature online presence. In other words, jobs are lost because job seekers did not manage their online presence.

On the other hand, social media, particularly LinkedIn, affords job seekers easy access to companies they may want to work for, hiring managers who work at those companies, and the ability to connect and develop a relationship with those hiring managers. Job candidates can use LinkedIn to research companies and interviewers prior to interviews to gain valuable insights that will better prepare them to interview well and secure a job offer.

Simplifying Social Media for Job Seekers

Unquestionably, there are volumes of resources on social media, online branding, and the hundreds of social media sites including Twitter, YouTube, Pinterest, and blogging sites. For the purposes of simplifying social media for your job campaign, and based on what I have discovered is most effective, I will focus attention on two main venues that I believe will enhance your opportunities for rapid employment: LinkedIn and Facebook.

LinkedIn

LinkedIn is the largest professional online social media site, closing in on 300 million members. Your LinkedIn profile is your online résumé! One of the main reasons LinkedIn is so important is that it is ranked VERY HIGH by all three major search engines. So when prospective hiring managers, HR professionals, and recruiters search your name on Google, Bing, or Yahoo!, your LinkedIn profile will most likely appear near the top of the first page. When I Googled my name at the time I wrote this section, there were 209 million results for Jay Block, and my LinkedIn profile was fourth! So even if you do not plan to actively engage in social media, you must have a strong presence on LinkedIn; this is NOT an option. The good news is that LinkedIn is free and easy to use, and you can transfer the information you have on your value-based résumé to create a good portion of your LinkedIn profile. Below I outline what you will need to create or enhance your own LinkedIn profile, and I include screenshots of a sample LinkedIn profile to help guide you. Feel free to open up your LinkedIn page and follow along.

To create a strong online presence using LinkedIn, you will need:

1. *A Professional Picture.* A good picture is imperative; not having a picture will significantly hinder your chances of being considered by hiring managers, recruiters, and HR professionals. The cliché says *a picture tells a thousand words*. But in today's online world, a picture tells 10,000 words! If you don't have a professional LinkedIn picture, rapid employment is virtually impossible.

2. *Your Professional Headline.* This appears under your name and should say what you do or are qualified to do and indicate the VALUE you represent to prospective employers (see the Ultimate Results messages discussed earlier in the chapter). This is important because studies show that hiring managers spend less than 10 seconds, on average, looking at the top of the profile to determine if the profile is worthy of additional consideration.

3. *Summary.* Your profile summary appears at the top of your profile just below the box with your picture and professional headline. This section is where you promote your skills and value. Here is where you can transfer the information on your résumé showcase to complete the LinkedIn Summary section. Not unlike the showcase of your résumé, the Summary section on LinkedIn should be brief, concise, and unique in that it communicates your value and quickly answers the questions, "Why should I hire you?" and "What can you do for our company?"

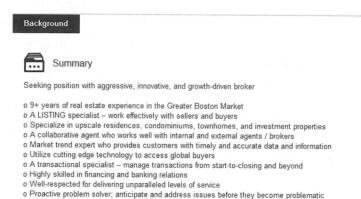

The rest of the LinkedIn profile consists of information that you have already completed on your value-based résumé. Sections that appear after the Summary include:

4. *Experience.* Use the information on your value-based résumé to complete this section. *Caution:* If you are employed and are seeking a new position, *I suggest you provide just your job description with your current employer and do NOT provide specific accomplishments.* Even in your job description, you want to be careful not to divulge specific information that, if your current employer saw it, might be construed as disclosing sensitive or confidential information while employed. For instance, if you manage an $8 million territory, it might be best to say you manage a multimillion dollar territory. Once you have left a company, you can provide specific accomplishments and statistics. But while you are employed, it is best, in most cases, NOT to mention specific accomplishments or any information that may lead your employer to suspect that you are seeking a new job.

Important note: LinkedIn is a professional social media site where professionals can meet and interact with other professionals to network, forge new relationships, and promote their personal brands. The vast majority of people on LinkedIn (over 90 percent) are currently employed. In fact, most employers expect their employees to be on LinkedIn to promote their companies and improve business and brand recognition. Indeed, Fortune 1,000 companies and their executives and employees, as well as small businesses, professionals, and enterprises of all makes and sizes, are well represented on LinkedIn. But if you are employed and are looking for a new opportunity, you'll want to take extra care in how you present yourself. You don't want to blatantly broadcast to your current employer that you are seeking a new job if your current employer happens to view your profile. If employed, you'll create your LinkedIn profile as if you had no intention of leaving your company, writing it in such a way that you promote your brand and your current employer—just like everyone else on LinkedIn who is employed.

 Experience

Real Estate Professional
Coldwell Banker United, Realtors
2012 – 2014 (2 years) | Beacon Hill, Boston

Specialized in residential and commercial real estate in Boston and the North Shore:
* Marblehead, Swampscott, Salem, Beverly

- Averaged $22 million a year in closings (Member: President's Club)
- Initiated "Young Professional Agents Facebook Group" and recruited 6 young top performers
- Elected Vice President of Back Bay Chamber of Commerce to enhance company's reach

Real Estate Professional
Century 21 New Millennium
2008 – 2012 (4 years) | Salem and the North Shore

Specialized in residential and commercial real estate in Salem and the North Shore:
* Marblehead, Swampscott, Salem, Beverly, Peabody, Wenham, Danvers, Topsfield

- Averaged $16 million a year in closings
- Awarded "President's Achievement Award" for exceeding production quotas
- Named "Team Player of the Year" by agents (26 agents vote for selection of this award)

Real Estate Sales Associate
Remax Alliance
2006 – 2008 (2 years) | Brookline

Began real estate career out of college and sold residential properties.

Worked under the tutelage of a senior broker the first year, Gorden H. Miller II (2006-2007). The team produced $25 million in sales that year.

- Selected "Rookie of the Year" 2006-2007 (Out of 12 new agents)
- Personally secured 7 listings and 8 new buyers for the team resulting in $8.7 million in sales
- Sold $8 million on first year as a solo realtor in 2008

5. *Education.* You can use the same information on your value-based résumé to complete this section, including continuing education, certifications, and licenses.

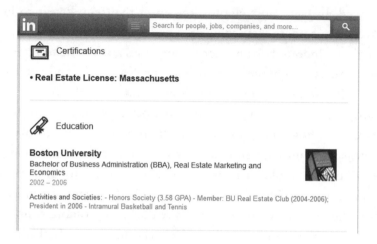

6. *Skills & Expertise.* This is a section where you can highlight your skills and areas of expertise to better help prospective employers understand what skills you are good at and your potential value to them. This is also an active section where your LinkedIn connections can endorse, or validate, the skills you list. You can list up to 50 skills that you feel will be most impressive to employers for the positions you are seeking in the Skills & Expertise section, but only 10 are prominently displayed. And honestly, very few hiring professionals have the time, or desire, to see 50 skills. Think back to the law of messaging introduced to you earlier in this chapter, where it explains that about six to eight things determine 90 percent of your value. The same law applies here. There are about six to eight areas of expertise that determine 90 percent of your value. And though it may seem redundant, your skills and expertise will now come from both the showcase of your résumé and the Summary section of your LinkedIn profile. Keep in mind that this is a section that must be clear and accurate in communicating those skills and areas of expertise that prospective employers most want to know you possess.

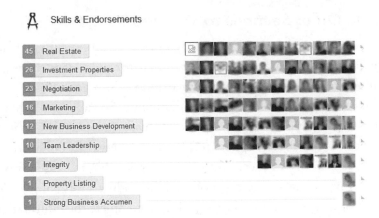

Skills & Endorsements

45	Real Estate
26	Investment Properties
23	Negotiation
16	Marketing
12	New Business Development
10	Team Leadership
7	Integrity
1	Property Listing
1	Strong Business Accumen

7. *Interests.* This section should be short and include only relevant interests that would be important to or resonate with hiring managers.

8. *Personal Details.* There are only two questions asked in the Personal Details section: your date of birth and marital status. I suggest that you ignore this section unless you have a strategic reason for including one or the other. Perhaps you feel that being married is advantageous to your campaign or that being single is a plus if the jobs you are seeking require prolonged travel. Simply use good judgment here. *Caution:* If you are going to include your birthdate, most online experts advise not to include your year of birth to protect you from potential identity theft. If you look at my profile, you will see I include my birthday (January 22) but not the year I was born.

9. *Advice for Contacting.* Oftentimes, people don't see the Contact Info section on the top of your profile. In this section, reenter your e-mail address and phone number to ensure that hiring managers and other potential employers know how to contact you.

 Additional Info

Interests

Physical fitness, tennis, golf, snow skiing, community activities (American Red Cross and Make-A-Wish Foundation), and family activities

Advice for Contacting William S.

Email: email@email.com
Phone: (781) 555-1212

Adding Other Sections to Your Profile

When you go into Edit Profile mode, you will see on the far right side of the profile an area called *Recommended for you*. Here there is a list of additional sections you can incorporate into your profile that are not part of the standard LinkedIn template. Sections you can add include Organizations, Volunteering & Causes, Languages, Certifications, Projects, Courses, Test Scores, Honors & Awards, Publications, and Patents. If any of these sections are applicable to you and will enhance your chances of getting noticed and landing a job, simply click on the + sign to the right of the sections and complete the information.

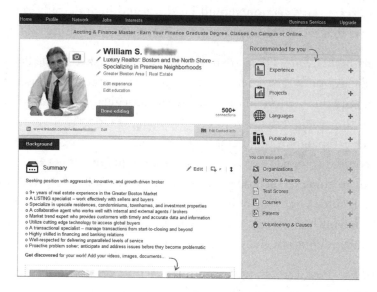

Once Your LinkedIn Profile Is Completed

Once your LinkedIn profile is completed, you can begin to expand your network and connect with employment agencies, recruiters, and hiring managers you have identified who are on LinkedIn. The larger your network, the more likely your profile will show up in search results pages. The more employment agencies and recruiters you have in your network, the better your chances are of getting discovered. Go to Advanced People search, and using the keyword "recruiter" or "employment agencies," add as many as you can. Most recruiters and employment agencies want to connect with as many job candidates as possible for their own database. If you do not want anyone (including your current employer, if you are employed) to see your connections, click on "Privacy and Settings" and then click on "Profile." You will see to the right a link that says "Select who can see your connections." Click on that and select "Only You." This way no one can see who you are connected to.

This next bit of advice can be uncomfortable for some. Connect with everyone—people you know and people you don't know! This is a professional venue. Personally, I connect with all who invite me to connect with them because I believe there is strength and power in numbers. As I approach 20,000 connections, I can reach more than 26 million people around the globe who are within two degrees of separation (directly connected to me or someone I am connected with who knows someone I need to meet). If "who you know matters," I have access to millions of people!

A few years back, I read a career industry book written by the chairman and CEO of a Fortune 500 company. I really wanted to speak to him. So I sent a message from my LinkedIn home page in the Share an Update section at the top the page and posted a message asking if any of my LinkedIn contacts knew this person. To my surprise, the next day, one of my LinkedIn connections responded to me and told me she had a LinkedIn connection who knew a person who worked directly for the person I wanted to speak with. Three days later, I was on the phone speaking to him.

Many people are skeptical about connecting with people they don't know. But don't you do this when you go to a chamber of commerce meeting? Don't you meet strangers and collect business cards with phone numbers, e-mail addresses, and other information when you attend networking events? Your LinkedIn profile is like an expanded business card and networking venue! The more connections you have on LinkedIn, the more people you have who can hire you or refer you to others who can hire you. And the more connections you have on LinkedIn, the more likely hiring managers and recruiters will take you seriously and trust you because they will view your large network as a sign that other people have confirmed that you are a job candidate worthy of getting to know.

Joining Groups

There are more than a million and a half groups on LinkedIn for every conceivable topic. There are LinkedIn groups for people who walk dogs (as a profession) and groups for millionaires. There are groups for specific professions and groups for specific industries. A LinkedIn group is where a number of people gather online around a common subject. If you are in retail, there are many LinkedIn retail groups. If you are in manufacturing, you could find a variety of manufacturing groups. If you are interested in a job in sports, there are many groups addressing almost every sport imaginable. There are two primary reasons for belonging to groups: (1) to facilitate discussions and (2) to access members of the group to communicate with and establish new relationships with. This is a good time to explain that LinkedIn is not a social media venue for spamming. In order to communicate by LinkedIn to other people, you must be LinkedIn (connected) with them. However, if you are a member of a group, you can communicate and send a message to all members of the group, whether you are actually connected on LinkedIn or not. I am not advocating that you become a job-seeking group spammer. What I am suggesting is that you strategically use groups to make new contacts, share information, build new relationships, and share your value with those who might benefit from what you have to offer, or who can refer you to those who might.

By participating in relevant and provocative group discussions, your name—or personal brand—will get noticed. If you were to spend just 5 to 10 minutes a day checking out your top three or four groups, commenting on other people's posts, or posting your own content-rich and job- or industry-relevant thoughts, you will get noticed. When you share your expertise and interact with others in groups that are in the industry in which you wish to land a job, you significantly expand your chances of doing just that because people you don't know and whom you could never have connected with in the past get to know you and interact with you. And they just might have a job opening or be able to refer you to someone who does.

Here is a strategy that most job seekers absolutely love—target connecting. You have unlimited access to all members of the groups you belong to! You do NOT have to be LinkedIn with members to send members of the groups you belong to a short message. Target connecting is a strategy where you join groups that have members who could possibly hire you, refer you to people who could hire you, or provide you with valuable information to that end. *This strategy requires tact and authenticity.* The message must be short and respectful and have value to the members you are sending the message to. Go to the group's member listing (some groups I belong to have 55,000–100,000 members!) and study the member profile summaries. If a member of the group appears to be someone who might be able to assist you, send a brief *personal* message, using the "send a message" link. An example might be:

> *Dear Mary,*
>
> *We are members of the LinkedIn Nursing Network group. I respect your time but wanted to quickly introduce myself as a possible nursing candidate with your hospital, knowing I would be a valuable asset. If an opportunity exists or might exist in the future, I would enjoy connecting with you. If there is anything I can do to assist you in any way, please don't hesitate to reach out.*
>
> *Thank you,*
>
> *Charlene Wilson*

You can use the same message for various people—a great off-hours strategy that would allow you to send out 25, 50, or more messages a day. However, you should take the time to personalize every message you send. Be brief, polite, and respectful of their time.

One of the goals I advocate when using LinkedIn and all other social media is to establish key connections and then invite those connections to engage in a telephone or Skype conversation. When you are able to get a LinkedIn connection on the phone or in a Skype conversation, you are on the fast track to your next job. Skype is a FREE Internet calling service that uses video to allow users to communicate with other people online. Skype is a very valuable tool for job seekers, as it allows them to communicate with anyone anywhere in the world using voice and video for free. Recently I made a valuable LinkedIn contact in Australia, and approximately every month we Skype and discuss topics of mutual business interest. She sees me, I see her, and there is a synergistic relationship that is easily established due to the power of visual communication. When you are able to make a connection and then elevate the relationship to a face-to-face or telephone relationship, you begin to make significant strides in achieving your goals.

Final Thoughts

LinkedIn research. LinkedIn allows you to perform research on companies, job openings, and people. At the top of the LinkedIn page, there is a white search box that reads "Search for people, jobs, companies, and more." By clicking on the arrow to the left of the box, a scroll-down menu bar will appear for people, jobs, companies, universities, groups, and articles. Just key in what you want to research, and you will be introduced to a plethora of data and information.

A *live e-mail signature line.* An easy way to drive people and prospective hiring managers to your LinkedIn profile is to have a live link in the signature section of your e-mail and on your smartphone and tablet. Whenever you send an e-mail, no matter where you send it from, I suggest you can have a live link that takes people directly to your LinkedIn profile.

> Warm regards,
>
>   Jay Block
>
>   LinkedIn: http://www.linkedin.com/in/jayblock

Do not upgrade. LinkedIn is free; you do not have to pay to have a profile or to use the standard applications I have covered in this section. However, at times, LinkedIn will attempt to entice you to upgrade and pay a monthly fee for some advanced applications. *Unless you have a very specific reason for justifying upgrading your account, you should never pay a fee for LinkedIn.* In all my years of helping job seekers conduct successful job campaigns, I have yet to meet a job seeker, at any level at any time, who needed to upgrade his or her account. Keep your credit card in your wallet!

You will never get a second chance to make a great first impression. We live in an online-connected world that includes a globally connected job market. Odds are that your first impression, or an important subsequent impression, will be established online. LinkedIn is the world's largest professional social network, and it is here, more than in any other venue, that employers seek out new talent and validate talent already identified. And it is here where your lasting impression will probably be made. You have full control over what employers see. You have full control over how you manage your image—your online impressions. And you have full control over whether you want to make the commitment to be professionally LinkedIn. It's easy to do. It's free. And it's an important strategy and tool for landing the job you want at the pay you deserve—quickly. If for no other reason, get LinkedIn because your LinkedIn profile is your online résumé.

Online but off-track. I have only highlighted some of the most important aspects of LinkedIn. It is important that you take advantage of the available resources and the tools and strategies offered by the largest professional online social networking venue in the world. Yes, you'll want to have a profile and be active in some strategic manner. But you'll also want to manage your time well so you don't waste your valuable resources of time and energy. You don't want to find yourself spending so much time on LinkedIn and other social media without getting the return on investment of your time and energy. The goal is to better understand and utilize LinkedIn and social media so you invest just the right amount of time to be effective in your job campaign.

Facebook

Rethink what you think you know. Facebook is not just for teenagers or social interaction. In fact, at the end of 2013, Facebook's chief financial officer, David Ebersman, said that teen usage of the social network had been declining but that business and professional pages were on the rise. Haven't you noticed how many companies advertising on television and elsewhere are ending their ads by asking their audience to "Like us on Facebook"? A major shift is taking place in social media in general and on Facebook in particular, and you can take full advantage of this shift to land a job quickly before millions of other job seekers catch on. The shift I am referring to is what I call *professionalizing your Facebook presence*.

Not so long ago, most employment professionals and hiring managers advised job seekers to keep their Facebook profiles separate from their professional profiles or even to keep them completely private. But Facebook's dominance as the giant of all social media can no longer be ignored in the employment sector. Furthermore, while recruiters and employment agencies are using Facebook more and more to find and screen job candidates, hiring managers are looking at Facebook profiles to assess the character and integrity of potential job candidates. And ahead-of-the-curve job seekers are positioning their value, brand, and personality to win jobs by showcasing themselves on their Facebook page. The concept of professionalizing your Facebook presence means you can't afford not to have a strong and professional presence on Facebook.

The law of averages is a constant force because of the monstrous reach that Facebook has—1 billion+ users. When you post something on your Timeline, that post may show up on many of your friends' home pages. And, of course, your friends' friends may also see your post if you manage your settings strategically. When you post comments on your friends' Timelines, their friends can also see your comments. Facebook's reach is stunning if you use it wisely to land a job, make more money, and secure your financial future.

I continue to be amazed at how many people misunderstand Facebook or are outright terrified by it. This comes primarily from not knowing how to properly use and optimize it. No one has to know your social security number, address, what you wear, where you go, whom you hang out with, or anything about your private life. When you understand how powerful Facebook can be when you professionalize your Facebook presence, not just in landing a job but keeping and growing in it, you'll come to realize that rethinking your beliefs about Facebook could be one of your greatest assets to rapid and long-term employment.

Facebook: The Third Largest Country in the World

If Facebook were a country, with over a billion users, it would be the third largest country in the world behind China and India. There are over 700 million people who log onto Facebook daily, 4.5 million "likes" generated daily (most for professional organizations or businesses), and there are more than 825 million mobile active users.* In Europe, over 225 million people are on Facebook,† and 7 new profiles are created every second;‡ and today an estimated 85 percent of all employment and hiring managers, when using social media as an assessment resource, look to Facebook to evaluate the professionalism and integrity of prospective job candidates.§

It is entirely up to you to embrace the shift or not. Yes, hiring managers will see the color of your skin, your approximate age, and other things that years ago may have been considered private and even illegal for employers to ask about. But technology has changed the entire landscape of the workplace, from hiring to firing and everything in between. If you decide to stay off Facebook, you risk losing job opportunities to job seekers who are professionally branding themselves throughout this most impressive empire.

So here's the deal: the process of *professionalizing your Facebook presence* begins with making the decision to use it wisely, strategically, and professionally. There is no need to be concerned that Facebook will ruin your life, your identity, and your privacy. Not unlike LinkedIn, if you only have professional information throughout your Facebook profile, what is there to be concerned about? Facebook is like an automobile. If you are prudent and responsible, it can be a valuable tool to help get you from where you are to where you want to go. But if you are reckless and irresponsible, it could cause great harm. You just have to pay attention and navigate with skill and common sense.

---

*Source: Facebook
† Source: *Search Engine Journal*
‡ Source: ALLFacebook
§ Source: National Association of Colleges and Employers

Two Strategies for Using Facebook

The first strategy I call *Facebook passive*. This means you create a professional look on your personal Facebook page, but you will NOT be active. This strategy ensures that if hiring managers, recruiters, referrals from friends, or anyone else for that matter visits or lands on your Facebook page to evaluate you for a potential job opportunity, you look highly attractive! Once your Facebook page is completed, all you have to do is check it every day or two for a few minutes to be sure your profile looks just the way you want it to look. That's it... just create it and manage it every once in a while.

The second strategy I call *Facebook active*. Obviously, this means you will create a professional look on your personal Facebook page, but you will be active by posting professional posts, finding industry-related articles and sharing the link to the articles on your Timeline, posting appropriate pictures, and connecting with other people to expand your brand and increase your sphere of influence—your network.

People hire and refer others to employers that they know, like, and trust. Facebook, unlike LinkedIn, allows you to portray yourself both in written form and in pictures. Everyone is different and will certainly have a different strategy. It is absolutely appropriate to integrate relevant social posts and pictures with professional posts and pictures. You can post a picture of yourself at a Race for the Cure event, of you and your spouse celebrating your anniversary, or even of your children, and have it be relevant and appropriate. My message here is this: be mindful of what you post and what pictures you insert. *Pictures are important on Facebook because Facebook, unlike LinkedIn, is first and foremost a visual site.* So always think about potential employers and ask, "Will prospective employers view this post or picture positively or negatively?"

Many Facebook-active job seekers choose to add and connect with friends (contacts) they don't know only after they have checked out their profiles to be sure they are professional and business-relevant. In other words, the strategy is that by accepting qualified friends that you don't know personally, you have added new potential employment contacts that could very well play a role in helping you land a new job. Similar to going to a local networking event, meeting strangers, and collecting their business cards, joining Facebook gives you access to a massive and unprecedented networking forum to build new contacts with hiring managers, recruiters, human resource professionals, and people who have the ability to refer you to potential job opportunities. And keep in mind that millions of companies, from small enterprises to Fortune 500 firms, have Facebook business pages. This provides job seekers with another tactical research venue to seek out information and contacts to secure rapid employment.

The choice is yours. You can choose not to engage in any form of Facebook activity, you could become Facebook passive, or you could be Facebook active. A great majority of the world's population and businesses spend so much time online that I believe optimizing your professional online presence is well worth the time and effort.

Personalizing Your Profile

You can insert two pictures atop your Facebook profile—what I call your first and lasting impressions. I suggest the profile picture, the smaller picture that is attached to every communication you send, be highly professional, perhaps the same one you used on LinkedIn. Your cover photo, the large banner behind your profile photo, is where you can showcase your industry, your profession, or your character. I believe both pictures, when combined, must make a powerful statement that communicates that you are a prime candidate worthy of being hired!

Your About Me section should be professionally presentable. I coach my clients to first work on and complete their LinkedIn profile. I recommend to most of my clients that they just copy and paste the LinkedIn Summary into the About Me section. There should be no "personal stuff" on the professionalized Facebook profile. Leave the "Relationship" section blank unless you have a reason for including your family members and are comfortable with doing so. There is a section for providing favorite quotes. If you have one that is relevant to landing a job, such as "Always go the extra mile," include it. If

your favorite quote is "An eye for an eye and a tooth for a tooth," it's probably best you leave that section blank! There are "Basic Information," "Places Lived," and "Contact Information" sections throughout your Facebook page. Fill in only what is directly relevant to landing a job. And don't fill in any sections or share information you are not comfortable with or that is not relevant to landing a job. For instance, there is a section where Facebook asks if you are interested in men or women and what your relationship status is. Remember, you are *professionalizing your Facebook presence.* Leave this blank! There is a section to share your religious and political views. I suggest you leave this blank. If the information you are sharing is not directly related to your value to the marketplace and the job market, just leave it blank!

Your News Feed

One of the primary concerns people might have about using Facebook as a professional tool has to do with the News Feed section. This is the section where your friends and contacts post about their grandmother's knee replacement surgery, where Marty is going for lunch, why the president should be impeached, and Aunt Mary's trip to Dunkin Donuts to meet her best friend Millie and her new dog Stroodles. By its nature, it is a very social section, and you might be concerned that potential employers will look through your News Feed and determine that you might not appear professional, in part because of what other people post.

The News Feed section is not visible to anyone else but you. Personally, I am *Facebook active*, and my strategy is to accept anyone who appears professional. I have well over 4,000 Facebook friends and don't personally know many of them. So you can imagine the variety of nonprofessional posts that appears on my News Feed! But I have so many Facebook friends because everyone I accept is a potential prospect or a referral source for me to increase business and earn more income. If I were a job seeker, these 4,000 friends (contacts) would be potential hiring prospects or referral sources for a job.

Because of my large amount of contacts, I have learned to filter the important posts on my News Feed. When I go to my News Feed, I allow myself only 10 minutes to scroll the page. I ignore anything that is not relevant to my business, identify a few potential business prospects, "like" their comments or post a comment of my own, and even reach out to those I'd like to get to know because they might be beneficial to my business. The same strategy works well for job seekers! This is a great way to create meaningful contacts that could lead to your next job. On those very few occasions where someone I am friends with turns out to be unprofessional, I have no problem unfriending him or her, and you shouldn't have a problem either!

The Facebook Tag

Friends and connections are able to create a link to your Timeline through a tag. When you are tagged in someone's picture or post, your profile is linked to this post unless you remove—or untag—yourself from the post.

When you visit my Facebook page, I know exactly what I want you to see and read. Sometimes family members and close friends will see an article or picture on Facebook that they feel I would want to see or read, and they *tag* me. Though it is usually appropriate and interesting, it is seldom the first impression I want prospective clients to see, so I untag myself and *hide it from my Timeline*. I still have access to it, but no visitor to my Facebook page can see it. You can do the same thing because you have control of what prospective employers, recruiters, and employment agencies see when they visit your Facebook page. Just by spending a few minutes a day monitoring your profile, you can ensure you have one that portrays you in a highly professional manner. There is also a setting whereby no one can tag you (or place a picture or post) on your Facebook page without your authorization.

To better understand the process of professionalizing your Facebook presence, I invite you to visit my Facebook page and explore all the areas of my site. This will give you a good idea of what I mean by "professionalizing your Facebook presence." Then feel free to invite me to become your friend!

Jay Block's Facebook Address:
https://www.facebook.com/JayBlockCareers

I have only highlighted what I consider to be the most important aspects of Facebook. You didn't drive a car well the first time you got behind the wheel; you had to practice and get lessons from a seasoned driver. The same is true of Facebook. I believe Facebook is too big and powerful to ignore. Study Facebook and ask for help from those who are proficient with it. Set your privacy settings to reflect what you feel comfortable showing the world. Take advantage of Facebook on your smartphone and upload photos from professional events that will enhance your professional image. If used correctly, Facebook can be an excellent rapid employment tool for most job candidates.

Time Management and Resource Optimization

Social media is one of a number of strategies you will use to land a job quickly, and we will explore the other strategies in the next chapter. I covered the two primary social media strategies that I believe 90 percent or more of all job seekers should consider utilizing in their job campaign—LinkedIn and Facebook. However, if you are an industry leader or are very well known in your profession, you may want to consider using other social media tools such as Twitter and blogging. These are social media venues for job seekers who have a well-established brand that prospective hiring managers and recruiters would recognize and follow. A number of job seekers have opted to create video résumés or YouTube videos, certainly a nontraditional strategy as well. A search for video résumés on YouTube will result in tens of thousands of candidates who have posted their video résumés for prospective employers to review. Many videos are well designed, while others are so poorly presented, they tend to sabotage any chance of impressing a hiring professional. The advantage of a video résumé is that very few people, percentagewise, have actually created one, so they serve as a differentiator in the recruiting process. The disadvantage is that if it is not well produced or you don't present yourself professionally, you won't have much of a chance to win an interview. A good video résumé is short, about two minutes, and addresses the same information we discussed for creating résumés: your value, skills and areas of expertise, and results you have produced in the past. An effective video résumé will quickly explain why you're the best person for the job and addresses your background in a storylike format. If you are a person who isn't comfortable in front of a camera, if you don't come across well in a video, or if you can't afford to produce a high-quality video, this is probably not an appropriate tool for you. If you are going to consider this option, ensure that the content and presentation are professional and that the subject matter promotes you in an effective way.

STEP 3 SUMMARY

■ Write a résumé that stands out from your competition. Your résumé must clearly communicate bottom-line results and organizational objectives you can produce that position you as a highly qualified and valuable candidate.

■ Write your résumé thinking about the interview. When you take the time to properly prepare your résumé, thinking about the key messages that will win you job offers, you'll then showcase those messages on your résumé to win interviews!

■ There are no rules for writing résumés! The goal of your résumé is to STAND OUT. You cannot distinguish yourself from other job candidates if you blend in with them. You must blow your own horn; your résumé is not the place to be humble!

■ Keep your résumé as brief as possible. Given the scores of résumés crossing the desks of hiring authorities, shorter is better. A one- or two-page résumé is the norm, but there are exceptions.

■ Be careful not to conduct the interview in the résumé or ask the reader to labor through pages and pages of "stuff." Be precise, stay on message, and keep your résumé effectively succinct.

■ Be sure your résumé is well organized and reader-friendly. The presentation should be crisp, exciting, and inviting.

■ When you have completed writing your résumé, test-market it! Identify five to seven people whose opinions you value and ask for their honest feedback. Also, when five to seven people read your résumé, this will assure you that there are no typographical or grammatical errors.

■ Don't embellish or lie. Be innovative and resourceful to get your foot in the door, but do so knowing you'd pass a lie detector test if you were asked about the truthfulness and accuracy of your résumé.

■ Your résumé must answer four critical questions. The first three must be answered in 15 to 20 seconds:

- What position(s) are you seeking or what are you qualified to do that would be of value to our company or organization?
- What results and contributions make you better than other qualified candidates?
- What skills, qualifications, and assets do you bring to the job that would lead us to believe you can produce the results you say you can produce?
- Can you provide specific results (achievements) that you produced in the past that would indicate that you can produce them in the future?

■ Know the law of messaging: there are about six to eight messages that you have to communicate that make 90 percent of the difference between getting and not getting an interview.

■ Create a "showcase" atop your résumé. It is in the showcase where you will send your powerful 15- to 20-second message communicating that you are a highly qualified job candidate! In the showcase, include:

- *The Ultimate Results messages.* The Ultimate Results messages communicate to prospective companies and hiring authorities your value, your worth to them—in other words, what you get paid to produce.
- *The Core Strengths messages.* Determine and reveal your six to eight core strengths that would lead a prospective employer to believe you can produce the Ultimate Results.
- *The Differential messages.* Differential messages communicate to prospective employers not only that you have the skills and qualifications to do the job better than other qualified candidates, but that you bring more to the job than what's required.

■ When you work on the employment section, you'll want to address two distinct components for each job or position that will appear on the résumé: (1) your detailed job responsibilities or job description and (2) your achievements and contributions—the results you produced.

■ Leave personal information, including age, place of birth, marital status, religious, political, and other possibly controversial activities or subjects, and other nonrelevant information off your résumé unless there is a strategic reason to include it.

■ As a rule, salary history is not included on résumés. If you are seeking a federal job or have other tactical reasons for including salary information, go ahead and include it.

■ You might want to consider including on your résumé the reasons for leaving places of employment. If you have had many jobs in a short period of time where you might be perceived as an unreliable job candidate, you may want to provide short, effective, and nondefensive reasons for leaving prior positions.

■ Don't underestimate the intelligence of hiring and employment professionals. Do not come across as devious, deceptive, or desperate.

■ In addition to formal education, employers want to know what you do to continually expand your knowledge and improve your professional skills. What continuing education courses have you attended? How many personal development seminars have you completed? How many professional improvement workshops have you attended? What computer skills are you proficient in? Let employers know you are a lifelong student of your vocation.

■ If you have military experience, thank you for serving your country. I urge you to present your military experience on your résumé as proudly as you wore the uniform.

■ If you have space on your résumé and want to include relevant activities and professional affiliations, do it.

■ Cover letters should be short, because most hiring authorities just don't have time to read lengthy cover letters. Cover letters should be personalized if possible.

■ The reference portfolio is the secret weapon of the job campaign and rapid employment. This tool is made up of professional references that will confirm and validate that the achievements and contributions you noted on your résumé are truthful and accurate.

■ Use social media as a strategic tool that will result in rapid employment. The majority of hiring managers, recruiters, and employment agencies use LinkedIn—virtually your online résumé—to find and recruit new employees. There are many applications LinkedIn provides you with to research companies and industries and to connect and network with people who can help you land the job you want.

■ Use Facebook as another key tactical tool for landing a job quickly. For many people, Facebook is misunderstood and misused. But when you professionalize your Facebook presence and create your Facebook profile for strategic employment purposes, you give yourself a significant advantage over other job candidates.

■ I believe 90 percent or more of all job seekers must incorporate LinkedIn and Facebook into their campaign strategy. About 10 percent may want to consider Twitter, blogging, video résumés, and YouTube video presentations. If you are in the 10 percent group, use these social media venues intelligently and strategically.

4

CREATING A METICULOUS ACTION PLAN

A Written Strategic Plan Is Your GPS to Rapid Employment

At this juncture of the job campaign, I hope that you're excited about the prospects of landing the job you want at the pay you deserve—quickly! I expect you have established and now know how to maintain a positive, energetic, and confident attitude; have identified a meaningful job or career objective that will inspire and enhance your life; and have created and stockpiled a powerful arsenal of communications and self-promotional tools to outmaneuver and outcompete your competition. The next step of the job campaign process is to take all this positive momentum and develop a Meticulous Action Plan (MAP) so you can pursue and land the right job quickly. Without question, this is the most neglected aspect of the entire job campaign—creating and implementing a written action plan.

Take Out Your GPS Device

Most of us have a global positioning system (GPS) device these days in our cars, on our smartphones, or as a separate handheld instrument. A GPS is a satellite-based navigation system that has many different applications. If you want to navigate your way around a golf course, GPS technology provides an accurate course map with "distances" to help you get from tee to green. If you travel somewhere you've never been to, the GPS will provide a road map and precise directions for getting from your starting point to your ultimate destination. However, one of the limitations to GPS technology is that it doesn't have the capability of providing you with a road map and directions to your next job. This means you have to create your own MAP!

Plans

Successful endeavors are, in most cases, a result of following well-thought-out written action plans. A new business enterprise achieves success because the owners had a well-conceived written business plan. The sports team achieves success because the coaches created a highly effective written game plan. Have you ever taken the time to think about all the written plans people come up with to achieve specific goals? There are written retirement plans, vacation plans, financial plans, lesson plans, floor plans, weight loss plans, battle plans, wedding plans, recovery plans, flight plans, and emergency preparedness plans. The truth of the matter is that when it comes to furthering your career, ensuring your family's financial well-being, and securing a meaningful and rewarding job, you need a written plan—a MAP. But if you're like almost 100 percent of all job seekers, you have no written strategy. And I remind you that *if you fail to prepare a written plan, be prepared to fail.*

The traditional ineffective and painful job search is made up of two primary steps: (1) write a cookie-cutter résumé that blends in with all the other résumés, and (2) wing it! Winging it normally involves two approaches, *click and pray* and *lick and pray*. Click and pray is where you sit at your computer for hours on end and click your résumé out to hundreds, if not thousands, of employers and recruiters, praying that someone will read your résumé and offer you that perfect job. Lick and pray occurs when you scour the classified advertisements and postings in newspapers and online to find jobs that interest you, place your résumé in an envelope and lick it shut, deposit it in the mailbox, and pray someone will contact you for a job opportunity. Not effective strategies!

And then there is the matter of how much time the average out-of-work person invests in these two strategies during the week. The average unemployed job seeker spends less than 12 hours a week trying to land a job! How can this be possible when one's financial future and well-being depend on becoming employed? Apparently the job search is so painful or instills such a personal sense of hopelessness that the average job seeker is only willing to spend 12 hours or less—out of 168 hours in a week—creating a better future. Why is this? One of the main reasons is that job seekers don't have a MAP—a written success strategy to follow. Step 4 will introduce you to 12 ways to land a job and how to best use your time so you take full advantage of the strategies available to secure rapid employment.

So let me pose a few questions to you. Do you know the 12 strategies to land a job? Do you know which of the 12 strategies will work best for you? How many hours a week do you plan to invest in designing your future and landing your next job quickly? What specific tasks will you work on each day? What are your goals for each week? The good news is that if you're willing to roll up your sleeves and work hard to complete the assignments I will ask you to do throughout this chapter, you will find that securing the job you want is not difficult at all. Once you have a well-designed MAP, you'll have a clear advantage over all your competitors who are spending less than 12 hours a week winging it!

This Is an Active Chapter

Simply reading this chapter won't help you much. The miracle of achieving rapid employment lies in completing the assignments presented in this chapter. If you are prepared to adjust your mindset as we covered in Step 1, this step will be enjoyable and life changing. This is not homework; rather, it's designing your future work. Once you have a plan of action that outlines daily tasks and weekly goals, you'll have created your own personal GPS that will direct you to your next job.

Actually, creating a MAP is more important than having a world-class résumé. As an example, let's take the case of Paul, who desperately needed a job. He had no résumé, but he did have a written strategy, which follows:

> *Wake up every weekday at 7 A.M., get dressed, and eat a good breakfast. At 9 A.M., head to Main Street and call on businesses on Main Street and in office buildings all day, with the goal of calling on 60 to 80 businesses a day to fill out employment applications to land a job. Return home, exercise every night for 45 minutes, and spend quality time with the family regardless of how the day went.*

That was Paul's written MAP. His strategy was to wake up early every morning and spend the entire day walking down Main Street going into every store and office building, filling out as many applications as he could, and meeting as may prospective hiring managers as possible. He also made the commitment to exercise and spend quality time with his family every evening. He knew he couldn't control whether he got a job; but he had total control over his health and family relations. On his fourth day, with tired legs and having overcome rejection after rejection, a company asked Paul to fill out an application, and he was hired two days later. Paul's strategy was the relentless pursuit of a job and a self-imposed demand that he call on 60 to 80 potential employers a day—or between 300 and 400 a week! How many people do you know who would do this? But Paul landed a job in a matter of days because he had a written plan, as simple as it was, and most importantly, he worked his plan every day!

Creating Your Meticulous Action Plan

Your MAP will be all encompassing and will address your entire week's activities. When you're done developing your action plan, you'll have a highly structured schedule of activities for each day of the week. This includes your job campaign as well as your personal, social, and fitness activities. MAPs are essential not only if you're out of work but also if you have a job and are seeking a better one. If you are out of work, you can invest 50, 60, or 70 hours a week in your job campaign. If you have a full-time job, you may only have 5, 10, or 15 hours a week to invest in a job campaign. Success is determined by (1) the number of hours you put into the job campaign and (2) the effort and activities you put into the hours.

> Whether you are employed and looking for a better job or out of work seeking a new one, you must hold yourself fully accountable for putting in as many hours as possible and getting the most out of every hour you put in.

How Many Hours a Week?

The first question you will need to address is, how many hours a week will you commit to your job campaign? If you are unemployed and must land a job quickly, 60 or more hours a week is not unreasonable. What else is more important if there's an urgency to get back to work? Personal responsibility and massive discipline are the two driving forces that will result in rapid employment. Demand of yourself that you work hard, stay focused, and raise the bar so high, no other job candidate will match your level of intensity and activity. When you work harder and smarter than your competition, you'll secure a new job with surprising ease in any kind of job market. If you currently have a job and are seeking a better opportunity, you must determine the number of hours you're able to invest each week. Ten hours is not unreasonable in most cases. Whether you are out of work or currently employed, at the end of each week, you must reflect upon (1) the time you invested, (2) the tasks you undertook in the time you invested, and (3) the goals you achieved. When you have a structured MAP, you'll have a powerful tool that will propel you to secure rapid employment.

How Many Hours a Day?

Based on the number of weekly hours you'll invest in getting a new job, your next step is to break weekly hours down into daily hours. Below is a conservative strategy that I suggest to those job candidates who are out of work and have an urgency to gain new employment. You have to determine for yourself how many hours you'll invest in your future—how badly do you want to land a new job? But for the purposes of this discussion, let's agree on 50 hours of weekly production time.

Number of hours a week: 50 hours

Monday	9 hours
Tuesday	9.5 hours
Wednesday	9 hours
Thursday	9.5 hours
Friday	9 hours
Saturday	Off
Sunday	4 hours
Total:	50 hours

The 12 Ways to Get a Job

There are probably hundreds of ways to get hired. However, there are 12 primary strategies available to most job seekers for landing a job.

Below I have placed the strategies in the order that "statistically" produces the best results—rapid employment.

1. Networking, New Contact Development, and Knocking on Doors

The U.S. Department of Labor confirms that between 60 and 85 percent of all jobs are secured through networking and contacts you have developed or will develop who can possibly hire you or refer you to people who can. Networking is, without question, the #1 way to get a new job. Bob Burg, author of *Endless Referrals*, says, "Effective networking is a matter of utilizing your natural sphere of influence, together with the one you are creating through networking skills, so that you will be referred to those who can help you quickly find the job you desire."

For the most part, you are not asking people in your network for jobs. You are asking people in your sphere of influence if they know of anyone in their network who can provide advice and information or refer you to people who can assist you to achieve your goal.

Based on every source available, every statistical analysis, and every research study ever performed, networking, both traditional and online (LinkedIn, Facebook, and other social media), is by far the most effective means to rapid employment. More than ever, it's who you know more than what you know.

■ *Networking / new contact development.* You are not "begging" people for a job or referrals. Change your thinking! Know that when you network effectively, you are actually creating your own personal sales force. For instance, if I am aware of your skills and abilities and can refer you to a company I know, confident that you can be of value to that company, I become a hero by putting you and the company together. Networking and adding new contacts to your network are success strategies because all parties benefit from the process!

■ *Knocking on doors.* Remember Paul's written strategy where he woke up every weekday at 7 A.M., got dressed, ate a good breakfast, and at 9 A.M. headed for Main Street to call on businesses all day? Well, this is the strategy known as *knocking on doors.* An analysis, released in 2012 by Jobs2web, Inc., of 1.3 million job applications revealed that *knocking on doors* or showing up at places of employment, whether there are positions available or not, has up to a 47 percent success rate. (Job seekers have only a 4 to 10 percent chance of landing a job through job postings on the Internet, according to this study). The important statistic to note here is that when job seekers come face-to-face with prospective employers (a method for establishing new contacts), they have almost a seven times better chance of securing rapid employment as opposed to sending out résumés.

■ *Job clubs.* Joining a formal job club (usually free or a nominal fee) is a strategy for job seekers that has *the highest success rate of all job campaign strategies.* Highly successful job clubs meet multiple times weekly and consist of job seekers who feed off one other and share their own contacts. They exchange job leads and share each other's job objectives with the group. Successful job clubs are led by knowledgeable job campaign facilitators who ensure the environment is empowering, positive, and action driven. The main difference between a typical support group and the successful job club is *action*. Members make calls to people they know on behalf of other members. Members go out with other members to make introductions for one another at prospective employers as well as at businesses and networking events. Indeed, a well-managed job club provides motivational support and a community for people who might otherwise be isolated and alone. A job campaign, like all successful campaigns, requires a team that is dedicated to everyone's success, and the right job clubs will lead to rapid employment for its members.

2. Target Marketing (Identifying Companies You Want to Work For)

Target marketing is a strategy for targeting specific companies or organizations you want to work for and proactively going after them! Compile a list of 50 to a 100 companies you'd be interested in working for. Then research the name of the hiring manager for each company (sales director, accounting manager, customer service manager, warehouse manager, CEO, etc.). Once identified, send the person a hard copy of your cover letter, résumé, and reference portfolio by overnight, two-day delivery, or first-class mail. Be prepared to follow up by sending follow-up letters. Many unsolicited résumé files sent by e-mail won't make it through the firewalls, will end up in spam files, or will be deleted. But nobody deletes an overnight or Priority Mail delivery package. In fact, people eagerly open them!

Susan J. Cook, former executive vice president and chief human resources officer for Eaton Corporation, has some pointers from an HR perspective:

> Don't send résumés to multiple people in the same organization. Identify one person who would be the ideal person to read your résumé and send it to that person. Be professional and respect the hiring manager's time. The important thing is to quickly communicate how you can benefit the company—that's all that matters. In most cases, you are just another unknown name to the hiring manager, so it's important that you quickly communicate how valuable you can be to their organization. Human Resources professionals welcome your résumés.

But you must be authentic and communicate what you can do for us that would demand our attention in about 15 seconds. So research the company thoroughly and know how you would fit in. If they have an open position or expect one to open soon, and you communicate your value clearly, chances are good that they will contact you.

3. Executive Search Firms and Employment Agencies

Executive search firms and employment agencies get paid to place qualified candidates in jobs. Normally, executive search firms place candidates in higher-level jobs, and employment agencies place candidates in low- to mid-range jobs, both permanent and temporary placements. The good news is that job candidates don't pay any fees. The not-so-good news is that executive search and employment firms, as a rule, do not actively seek to place candidates; rather, they actively seek to fill client openings. A common misconception is that recruiters and employment agencies are the personal placement agents for job candidates. They are not. They receive job vacancies from client companies and then find appropriate candidates to fill those slots—thus the term *headhunter*. Some agencies specialize in specific occupations, while others are more general. The best strategy regarding executive search firms and employment agencies is to incorporate them in your campaign strategy, but don't count on them to be your savior!

Today, more and more companies are opting to "lease" employees from executive recruiters and employment and staffing agencies for a variety of reasons, for example, to save on health benefit costs or to just test-drive new employees for a period of time before hiring them (temp to perm). Even at the executive level, many companies are going in this direction, so it is a good strategy to consider contacting and connecting with targeted agencies and headhunters. That said, it is important that you understand that *high-end* executive recruiters, both contingency and retained, are contracted by client companies to identify and recruit *top talent* for key positions. Client companies pay executive recruiters up to 40 percent of a new hire's annual salary, and therefore, companies expect executive recruiters to identify and introduce high-caliber and extremely well-qualified candidates.

It's important to understand that unless you are a highly experienced candidate for positions that headhunters are seeking to fill, chances are you won't be a top contender or be considered at all.

4. One-Stop Career Centers (also referred to as American Job Center Network)

One-Stop Career Centers are a group of federal, state, and local offices that support economic expansion, assist job seekers (mostly unemployed) in securing employment opportunities, and train and develop talent to meet the skills, qualifications, and needs of the nation's employers. One-Stop Career Centers are part of the U.S. Department of Labor that works in partnership with employers, educators, and community leaders to foster economic development and high-growth opportunities in regional economies. This network exists to help businesses find qualified workers and to help workers find appropriate employers to meet their mutual needs.

There are more than 3,000 One-Stop Career Centers located in all 50 states and Puerto Rico. One-Stop Career Centers place a multitude of resources for businesses and for job seekers under one roof. They assist job seekers with résumés, access databases with available job openings, provide computer and Internet service access, and invite guest speakers to address job seekers on all aspects of conducting a successful job campaign. The typical One-Stop Center serves thousands of individuals who are seeking employment, changing jobs, reentering the workforce, or learning new skills. To start working with a One-Stop Center or to find out more about the services the centers offer, visit one near you, go to http://www.servicelocator.org, or call 877-US2-JOBS.

5. Internet Searches and Postings

You can use online job boards, which have access to millions of job openings posted by hiring companies and recruiters, and they provide venues to post your résumé as well. Job candidates can enjoy many attractive benefits including online profiles, free résumé postings, and e-mail job alerts. In addition, most organizations now feature fully operational career sites that function much like online job boards.

They also allow you to create profiles, post résumés, subscribe to alerts, and respond to job openings. Hundreds and hundreds of job boards and postings are available that serve a wide range of industries and professions. Some of the top sites include Monster.com, Careerbuilder.com, glassdoor.com, jobdiagnosis.com, USAJobs.gov (federal job board), Idealist.org (nonprofit job board), indeed.com, TheLadders.com (six-figure-plus job board), beyond.com, Simply Hired.com, LinkedIn.com, bright.com, snagajob.com, and dice.com (tech job board).

Online communities, both large and small, are forums where like-minded individuals interact with each other. The large communities cater to millions of individuals with features such as news, job openings, and company profiles. Smaller communities function as e-groups and e-lists, where members interact with each other on various issues. Executive recruiters and human resource professionals sometimes target these groups to post openings and solicit résumés. Additionally, online newspapers provide access to their employment classifieds and also to custom-designed job boards.

Websites of industry associations function much like professional communities. In addition to providing links to members, they often offer forums, job boards, networking opportunities, and event announcements. If you are in a profession or vocation supported by strong industry associations, association websites will offer yet another vehicle to help you land your next job.

Caution: Conducting an online job campaign can be an effective strategy. However, be aware that when you conduct an online campaign, you may be exposing yourself to potential privacy risks. Your job campaign becomes transparent and is open to scrutiny by almost anyone. Always protect your personal information, and avoid disclosing your social security number and any confidential information. Know also that there are many employment scams and charlatans out there seeking to take advantage of job seekers' vulnerabilities, so be alert and use common sense and wise discretion. And if you are employed, use extra caution if you don't want your current employer to find out that you're looking for a new job. Extra care must always be taken, if this is the case, in all aspects of your campaign.

Controlling what you can control is a job campaign success strategy. When you are proactive and manage activities over which you have control, such as networking, knocking on doors, identifying viable recruiters and employment agencies, and implementing target marketing, rapid employment is virtually assured. You can follow up, gather names, and seek out additional advice and information to be active in the campaign process. That said, millions of job seekers are simply competing for jobs posted online or are posting their résumés online in hopes that prospective employers will find them. It's almost like playing the lottery. So, yes, buy a ticket and spend some time with online strategies. But I recommend you don't invest an unreasonable amount of time relying on activities you over which you have little or no control.

6. Classified Advertisements in Newspapers and Trade Journals

What used to be the primary method of securing employment is quickly going the way of the pay phone. Yes, newspapers are still delivered and are available online, so this is another stone you don't want to leave unturned. But you also don't want to rely solely on this strategy. I do suggest you get the Sunday newspaper and scan the classified section. But better yet, scan the entire newspaper and identify which companies are placing large ads. They may be good prospects for target marketing. Read the business section and identify potential companies you may want to pursue. Be proactive, perform in-depth research, and go after companies that seem to be doing well and that interest you.

7. Federal Jobs

Preparing a job campaign to land a federal job is different from preparing a job campaign in the private and nonprofit sectors. Kathryn Troutman, one of the nation's leading experts in federal job transitioning and author of *Ten Steps to a Federal Job*, says:

> Federal jobs are available across the U.S. and offer competitive salaries and benefits. No matter what your expertise or where you live, if you want a job where you can develop your professional skills and make a

difference in the lives of others, check out federal employment. It's easy to find federal job announcements for any city in the United States and around the world at: www.usajobs.gov. You can search for jobs by geographic location, salary and job type.

In most cases, federal, state, and local government jobs take more time to fill, and there is intense competition because the jobs are more widely posted than other jobs. There is also fierce competition from current government employees seeking new positions internally. If this is one of the directions you want to go in, be aware that due to the sheer number of résumés government jobs attract, keyword software is utilized for résumé and application screening. So it is important that you have the right keywords and phrases on your résumé and application that match the specific jobs you are applying for. Yes, there are many federal and governmental jobs available. But I suggest you study and become highly familiar with the intricacies of applying for federal and other government positions. This will help you land a federal job sooner.

8. Blogs with Job Listings

Today a good majority of people subscribe to blogs to receive information based on interests and relevant activities. Blogs help people obtain timely information to keep them updated on emerging or declining industry and market trends, as well as material and data that will help them make better decisions to achieve their goals. Recently, larger blogs are integrating job banks into their websites, and thus subscribing to blogs is becoming a new and emerging job campaign strategy you may want to consider. Be sensible about the amount of time you spend reading blogs and responding to blog-related job posts to ensure that the time you do invest is directly related to landing a job rapidly.

9. College Career Departments and Alumni Associations

The primary goal of a college career department is to provide students and alumni with the tools and skills they need to launch successful job campaigns. Though many institutions place more emphasis on inviting companies on campus to recruit students, more schools are beginning to teach the art of self-marketing and the job campaign process. Many college and university alumni associations are beginning to see the value of offering career services to assist alumni who are out of work or who are seeking better jobs. This results in a win-win situation where alumni associations provide career assistance, which, in turn, ensures that alumni contributions and donations keep rolling in.

10. Job Fairs

Job fairs are a common method of entry-level recruiting and initial screening. They seldom provide a venue for significant mid- to upper-level jobs. For the corporate recruiter, they offer an opportunity to reach the most candidates in the shortest possible amount of time. For many students and entry-level candidates, job fairs provide an opportunity to meet with multiple employers in the same day. That being said, one of the best strategies when attending job fairs is not so much to hand out résumés but to collect as many business cards from the recruiters as possible. Then, take the business cards home, write a short, personal cover letter, and submit a hard copy of your résumé and reference portfolio by mail or overnight delivery. This way you STAND OUT from the rest of the crowd, and your résumé is not part of the job fair stockpile.

Personal Note: It has been my experience that most job fairs offer jobs for entry-level, minimum-wage, and commissioned personnel. The ones I have attended over the years are well represented by the military, vocational schools, and career assistance organizations. I am not suggesting that you ignore job fairs. However, when a job fair is advertised, carefully read the list of companies that will be attending and then assess if they are the kind of companies that will offer the type of jobs you want.

11. Volunteer Work

When you volunteer, you feel better about yourself. You are doing something worthwhile when you help to improve the quality of life of others. And when you volunteer, you have the opportunity to make new contacts that just might help you identify and land your next job. Zig Ziglar said, "You can get anything you want out of life, if you help others to get what they want out of life."

12. Creative Self-Marketing

Creative self-marketing is just that—something that is unique, conceivably outrageous, and different. Maybe you have the financial resources (and courage) to place your résumé in the newspaper as a full-page ad. Perhaps you have the financial resources (and courage) to purchase space on a billboard on a well-traveled road and advertise the position you are seeking. Possibly you can offer to work for a company for a month or two without pay to prove your worth. There is no limit to human creativity and resourcefulness. Creative self-marketing is simply "out-of-the-box" thinking about how best to land a job in unconventional ways.

Selecting the Strategies That Are Best for You

Most likely, you won't use all 12 strategies. The strategies you decide to use will depend on the economy, your marketplace, the competition, your personality, finances, and other considerations. Most effective action plans will incorporate 4 to 6 strategies. Your plan may include just 3 strategies or perhaps 8. Ultimately, you must customize a MAP that will work best for you. So review the 12 strategies and determine which 4 to 6 strategies (or as many or as few as you deem appropriate) will work most effectively for you. *Warning: Do not select strategies that are the easiest or most convenient.* Select those that, by working hard on them, will land the job you want quickly. Campaigns are not about easy; they're about outcome. Now, let's return to the weekly and daily hours discussed previously.

> *Number of hours a week: 50 hours*
> Monday   9 hours
> Tuesday   9.5 hours
> Wednesday   9 hours

Thursday	9.5 hours
Friday	9 hours
Saturday	Off
Sunday	4 hours
Total:	50 hours

The next step is to determine what strategies you will undertake during the hours you allocate to your job campaign. Below is an example of how to do this.

Example

Rebecca is a real estate sales associate who lost her job. She chose to transfer her skills from real estate sales to healthcare sales. Rebecca studied the 12 job campaign strategies and determined she would use 6 of them. She committed to working 50 hours a week on her job campaign and decided to invest her time in the following way:

Networking	30%	15 hours a week
Target marketing	20%	10 hours a week
Internet activities	30%	15 hours a week
Employment agencies	5%	2½ hours a week
Classified advertisements	5%	2½ hours a week
Volunteer work	10%	5 hours a week
Total:	100%	50 hours a week

Rebecca identified which strategies would produce the best results for her job campaign and determined how many hours to invest in each strategy. Now she needs to determine when, during the week, she will work her 15 hours of networking, 10 hours of target marketing, 15 hours of online work, 2½ hours with employment agencies and another 2½ on the classified ads, and 5 hours volunteering. Rebecca has come up with the following weekly action plan.

Rebecca created a plan showing how she will spend her time and on what strategies for each day of the week. The plan can always be modified and tweaked. But the objective is to produce a comprehensive MAP made up of specific activities that must be worked on every day to achieve the desired goal of landing a job quickly and methodically.

50 HOURS PER WEEK						
	Networking	Tar. Mkt.	Internet	Agencies	Classifieds	Volunteer	Total
Mon	3	4	2	0	0	0	9
Tue	4	0	4	1.5	0	0	9.5
Wed	4	4	1	0	0	0	9
Thu	4	2	2.5	1	0	0	9.5
Fri	0	0	4	0	0	5	9
Sat	Off	Off	Off	Off	Off	Off	Off
Sun	0	0	1.5	0	2.5	0	4
	15	10	15	2.5	2.5	5	50

Taking Care of You Is Job #1

While conducting your job campaign, it is critically important that you take care of you first—physically and emotionally. So the next step is to construct a highly structured weekly schedule that combines your job campaign efforts with activities not related to the job campaign, such as fitness, family time, and personal and social activities. Keep in mind that everything affects everything else. In the midst of a job campaign, you want to keep healthy and upbeat, to remain engaged with family members and friends, and to enjoy your hobbies and favorite activities to the extent that you can. If you enjoy golf but are on a tight budget, maybe you can play a round of golf once a month rather than every week, but practice once a week at the driving range to conserve your money. If you enjoy yoga but can't afford to go to class three times a week, maybe you can go once a week and find a yoga program online and practice at home the other two days until you land your next job and can return to the ideal regimen. You want to eat well, exercise every day (even if it's only a 30-minute walk), and stay happily engaged with family members and friends. Your structured weekly schedule will include both personal and job campaign activities. Look closely at Rebecca's structured weekly schedule below, and see how she successfully integrated personal and job campaign activities.

	Monday	Tuesday	Wednesday
7:00	Exercise	Exercise	Exercise
7:30	Exercise	Exercise	Exercise
8:00	Breakfast	Breakfast	Breakfast
8:30	Shower/dress	Shower/dress	Shower/dress
9:00	Target mkting	Networking	Networking
9:30	Target mkting	Networking	Networking
10:00	Target mkting	Networking	Networking
10:30	Target mkting	Networking	Networking
11:00	Target mkting	Agencies	Networking
11:30	Target mkting	Agencies	Networking
Noon	Target mkting	Agencies	Networking
12:30	Target mkting	Internet	Networking
1:00	Lunch	Internet	Lunch
1:30	Lunch	Lunch	Lunch
2:00	Networking	Lunch	Target mkting
2:30	Networking	Networking	Target mkting
3:00	Networking	Networking	Target mkting
3:30	Networking	Networking	Target mkting
4:00	Networking	Networking	Target mkting
4:30	Networking	Family time	Target mkting
5:00	Family time	Family time	Target mkting
5:30	Family time	Family time	Target mkting
6:00	Family time	Family time	Family time
6:30	Family time	Internet	Family time
7:00	Family time	Internet	Family time
7:30	Internet	Internet	Family time
8:00	Internet	Internet	Family time
8:30	Internet	Internet	Internet
9:00	Internet	Internet	Internet

Thursday	Friday	Saturday	Sunday
Exercise	Exercise	Sleep late	Exercise
Exercise	Exercise	Sleep late	Exercise
Breakfast	Breakfast	Sleep late	Classifieds
Shower/dress	Shower/dress	Sleep late	Classifieds
Target mkting	Volunteer	Breakfast	Classifieds
Target mkting	Volunteer	Shower/dress	Classifieds
Target mkting	Volunteer	Yoga class	Classifieds
Target mkting	Volunteer	Yoga class	Family time
Agencies	Volunteer	Yoga class	Family time
Agencies	Volunteer	Yoga class	Family time
Internet	Volunteer	Family time	Family time
Internet	Volunteer	Family time	Family time
Lunch	Volunteer	Family time	Family time
Lunch	Volunteer	Family time	Family time
Networking	Lunch	Family time	Family time
Networking	Lunch	Family time	Family time
Networking	Internet	Family time	Family time
Networking	Internet	Family time	Family time
Networking	Internet	Alone time	Family time
Networking	Internet	Alone time	Family time
Networking	Internet	Alone time	Family time
Networking	Internet	Alone time	Family time
Family time	Internet	Alone time	Family time
Family time	Internet	Alone time	Family time
Family time	Family time	Alone time	Family time
Family time	Family time	Time w/friends	Family time
Internet	Family time	Time w/friends	Internet
Internet	Family time	Time w/friends	Internet
Internet	Family time	Time w/friends	Internet

Your Action Plan Is Your Boss

If you are out of work, your job campaign must be a full-time activity. If you are currently employed seeking a new job, your job campaign must be treated like a part-time job. In both scenarios, you are the transition technician, and your MAP is the boss! When you look at Rebecca's weekly plan, almost every minute of the week is accounted for. Does this seem overly structured to you? It is this kind of structured discipline that leads to rapid employment. Of course, there is room for flexibility. You may need to rearrange your schedule as things come up from time to time in the course of a week. But at the end of the week, your boss (your MAP) requires that you work so many hours on specific strategies to achieve targeted goals. Do not let yourself off the hook. If anything, do more than the boss expects!

Goal Setting

All the planning in the world will lead you nowhere if you don't have clearly defined goals. Jim Cathcart, author and executive coach, said, "Most people aim at nothing in life and hit it with amazing accuracy." However, when you create your MAP, you create a big target you can aim at and hit with amazing accuracy!

Once you have a structured weekly schedule, you must set goals that you want to achieve from your weekly activities. I have five principles for setting goals and securing rapid employment:

1. *Set the bar high.* Resist the easy button. *Choose "mastery" over "easy"* and know that great accomplishments don't come from low expectations.
2. *Be realistic.* You want to set the bar high, but not so high that your goals are merely impossible dreams. *Don't ever settle for less, but be realistic when setting the bar high*, especially when it comes to timelines and deadlines. Make it challenging but not unrealistic.
3. *Don't cave in.* It's easy to get distracted. It's easy to let influences pull you away from your structured weekly schedule in

pursuit of your goals. Discipline and resolve will lead to rapid employment.

4. *Don't substitute.* Carroll O'Connor, the actor who played the role of Archie Bunker in the sitcom *All in the Family*, said that the problem for most people is that when they meet resistance in pursuit of their goals, they substitute easier goals rather than create better plans. When you meet resistance in pursuit of your goals (and you will), don't substitute easier goals; rather, become more resourceful and create a more refined plan; or work harder at the one you have.

5. *Celebrate.* When you achieve goals, celebrate! You work hard to achieve your goals, so when you achieve your weekly objectives, celebrate. If your goal is to send out 50 résumés a week and you meet that goal, celebrate even though you haven't landed a job yet. You are celebrating the achievement of sending out 50 résumés. When you celebrate, you appreciate and honor your own efforts. And when you begin to fully appreciate and honor your own efforts, you will quickly achieve the goals to which you aspire.

Rebecca's Goals

Rebecca's goals are outlined in detail below. These goals are based on the structured weekly schedule she created earlier.

Weekly goals

- 5 new contacts referred by people in my network
- 2 new contacts made on my own
- 3 to 5 follow-up communications from contacts made the previous week
- 3 to 5 follow-up communications from contacts made in the last month
- 1 message posted to all contacts via my LinkedIn and professional Facebook sites
- Check for new job clubs in my area

Target marketing

- 15 unsolicited résumés to be sent out

- 10 to 15 follow-up letters and e-mails for résumés sent out last week
- 15 to 20 follow-up letters and e-mails for résumés sent out in the past month
- 5 phone calls or in-person visits to companies I'd really like to work for

Internet

- Review positions posted on Craigslist, Monster.com, hotjobs. yahoo.com, and Careerbuilder.com
- 25 résumés submitted online
- 10 or more postings on job boards; update existing postings
- Update my own LinkedIn and professional Facebook sites

Employment agencies

- 3 to 5 contacts
- 3 to 5 follow-up communications (letters, e-mails, or faxes)

Classified advertisements

- 1 to 3 résumés to be sent responding to ads seen in online and newspaper classified employment sections
- 3 to 5 résumés to be sent out unsolicited based on scanning the entire Sunday newspaper

Volunteer

- Have fun and contribute in a meaningful way to a cause I believe in
- Meet as many new people as I can and authentically establish new relationships

Personal

- Enjoy every day and smile throughout the day no matter what
- Reward myself with a glass of wine only after I achieve my daily goals
- Walk 45 minutes every morning, 6 days a week

- Read a spiritual book 30 minutes every night before I turn on the television
- Call a friend at the end of every day to stay "connected"
- Have a "fun night out" every Saturday night with my spouse and friends
- Limit television (or eliminate it completely); watch only uplifting shows
- Eat well, take vitamins, and stay energetic and fit

Suppose I asked you to play a sport you never heard of. You arrive on the field, and I give you dozens of activities you have to do, but I don't tell you the goal of the game. If you don't know the goal of the game, how can you possibly win? If you have a structured weekly schedule but no goals, how can you possibly land a job quickly? So the final and most important part of designing an inspiring, high-impact MAP is setting specific goals.

Just as Carroll O'Connor suggested, if your goals are not being attained, you don't compromise or give up on your objective of landing a job; you modify your plan. And the action plan is your road map or "ticket" to your next job. The great Italian painter and sculptor, Michelangelo, said, "I hope that I always desire more than I can accomplish." Put your desires in writing, set the bar high, and follow the five principles of goal setting. When you do, you'll start receiving job offers sooner than you thought possible!

Assignment: It is now time for you to put quality time into creating your own customized MAP. Please go back and review the 12 strategies, and then prepare a plan that you will commit to and enjoy executing!

My MAP

Number of hours per week: (   )

Number of hours per day: (   )

- Monday   (   )
- Tuesday   (   )
- Wednesday   (   )
- Thursday   (   )
- Friday   (   )
- Saturday   (   )
- Sunday   (   )

List strategies	% of time	Hours per week per strategy
■		( )
■		( )
■		( )
■		( )
■		( )
■		( )
■		( )
	100%	( ) hours per week

Once you have identified the specific strategies you will use to conduct your job campaign, determine the percentage of time you want to devote to each strategy. Then you can determine the number of hours a week you will work at each. For instance, suppose you plan to invest 60 hours a week on your campaign, and 25 percent of that time will be spent on networking; 25 percent of 60 hours is 15 hours. If you are employed and can only invest 9 hours a week on your campaign where 60 percent will be spent working with executive recruiters and 40 percent networking, you'd spend 5½ hours on the former and 3½ hours on the latter.

Structured Weekly Schedule

Create your own personalized structured weekly schedule so you have a well-thought-out plan of action, knowing exactly what tasks you will perform each day. Include job campaign, personal, fitness, social, and all weekly activities.

Weekly goals

Strategy #1

■

■

■

■

Strategy #2

■

■

■

■

Strategy #3

■

■

■

■

Strategy #4

■

■

■

■

Strategy #5

■

■

■

■

Strategy #6

■

■

■

■

Don't Ignore the Tough Stuff

It stands to reason that you will create and modify your MAP based on many different variables, such as your finances, health issues, geography, market economics, and personality. But in the event your plan doesn't produce the results you want as quickly as you anticipate, you need to anticipate and be proactive by creating a "Plan B"—planning for a possible worst-case scenario.

	Monday	Tuesday	Wednesday
7:00			
7:30			
8:00			
8:30			
9:00			
9:30			
10:00			
10:30			
11:00			
11:30			
Noon			
12:30			
1:00			
1:30			
2:00			
2:30			
3:00			
3:30			
4:00			
4:30			
5:00			
5:30			
6:00			
6:30			
7:00			
7:30			
8:00			
8:30			
9:30			
10:00			

Notes:

Thursday	Friday	Saturday	Sunday

Yes, it is vitally important to remain in a positive, optimistic, and enthusiastic state of mind. This was thoroughly discussed in Step 1. But we all know that bad things can happen to good people and that Murphy's law is real! So here's a good campaign philosophy to adopt: *expect the best, but plan for the worst.*

Create the most powerful, aggressive, and results-driven MAP you can to quickly land the job you want and deserve. But also spend some time thinking about the worst-case scenario. This would include taking an honest look at your finances and planning how best to navigate through a longer-than-expected campaign. Be open with family members and friends, and muster the courage and resilience to face what must be faced to best serve and protect you and your family if things don't go exactly as planned. To effectively address the worst-case scenario, you might include seeking out employment professionals and professional help in any area that might affect your ability to launch a hard-hitting and effective job campaign. You might need to consider moving in with relatives for a short period of time to save money. Not ideal, but a possible bridge to your next opportunity. You might have to find a part-time job even though this is not high on your "this-is-what-I-want-to-do" list.

Perhaps you need to develop a life downsizing plan. Just as many businesses are downsizing, so must many individuals and families. This doesn't have to be painful. Can't you have fun figuring out how to cut back on things you really don't need or use so you can put more money in your pocket instead of lining the pockets of others? Ask yourself, "How can I downsize my life, enjoy the process, and still live a good-quality life?" If you ask that question with the sincere desire to answer it, you'll come up with some creative and workable answers.

An effective action plan does not ignore potential obstacles. You can't ignore potential hurdles that might be a barrier to employment. I previously shared with you the law of ignoring, which says that whatever you ignore will, in most cases, get worse in time or will come back to bite you in the you-know-where. Any number of obstacles might exist, including insufficient experience, educational and academic deficiencies, a lack of specific skills, the real but never admitted discriminations (age, disability, gender, race, etc.), an extended absence from the workplace, or an erratic work history. You must address and neutralize these obstacles. If you are not sure how to accomplish this, seek out counsel from job coaches, employment professionals, trainers, books, and timely and relevant information found online (keeping in mind that there is an abundance of antiquated information and misinformation online).

Anything is possible if you are committed to it! A MAP that is well conceived and strategically developed will become your GPS to your next job. When you know what you are going to do and accomplish every day of every week, your job campaign won't last very long. Yes, "winging it" is a strategy: getting up every day with no plan and hoping for the best. It's just not a good one; in fact, it usually results in an unnecessarily long and painful job campaign. You should be excited and confident knowing that if you put the time and energy, the thought and enthusiasm, into designing a customized MAP, you will be light-years ahead of your competition. Better yet, you'll be enjoying your first annual performance review while your competition is still clicking, licking, and praying!

STEP 4 SUMMARY

■ When it comes to ensuring your family's financial well-being and securing a meaningful and rewarding job, you need to create a written action plan: a MAP (Meticulous Action Plan). When you create a MAP, you are actually programming your own "employment GPS" so you can go from where you are to where you want to be.

■ When you're done creating your action plan, you'll have a structured schedule of activities for each day of the week. This includes your job campaign as well as your personal, social, and fitness activities.

■ If you are unemployed, you should invest 50, 60, or 70 hours a week on your job campaign. If you have a full-time job, you need to set aside a defined number of hours every week as an investment in your future.

■ The first question you will need to address is, how many hours a week will you commit to your job campaign? Then, based on the number of weekly hours, your next step is to break weekly hours down into daily hours.

■ There are 12 primary job campaign strategies for landing a job quickly Your job is to determine which 4 to 6 strategies will be most effective for you.

1. Networking, new contact development, and knocking on doors
2. Target marketing (identifying companies you want to work for)
3. Executive search firms and employment agencies
4. One-Stop Career Centers (also referred to as American Job Center Network)
5. Internet searches and postings
6. Classified advertisements in newspapers and trade journals
7. Federal jobs
8. Blogs with job listings
9. College career departments and alumni associations
10. Job fairs
11. Volunteer work
12. Creative self-marketing

■ Once you have identified which job transition strategies will work best for your campaign, determine when, during the week, you will work on each. You want to create a structured weekly schedule and have a detailed plan with specific daily tasks both for your job campaign and for personal and social activities.

■ A MAP without specific goals is not an effective plan. You will want to set specific goals for each strategy so you can track your success or modify the MAP if you are not achieving your weekly goals.

■ Have a "Plan B." Prepare for the worst-case scenario. It is important to remain in a positive, optimistic, and enthusiastic state of mind. But sometimes your plan won't come to fruition as quickly as you'd like. So expect the best, but plan for the worst.

TAKING ACTION

Master a Few Self-Marketing Skills... Then
Take Massive Action to Land a Job Quickly

"**P**ut your money where your mouth is." "Actions speak louder than words." "It's not what you say, it's what you do." This last step, Step 5, is what I call "the miracle piece to rapid employment." If you have a positive attitude, a well-defined goal, a strong résumé and other communication tools, and a well-thought-out action plan, but you take no action, you get no results—no new job. Contrary to popular belief, knowledge is not power. Knowledge is potential power. *Wisdom uninvested in labor is wasted!* The fact is, rapid employment and job campaign success come from taking action on what you know.

Take Action and Establish Your Campaign Headquarters

Do not underestimate the importance of having an inspiring place from which to conduct your job campaign. You want to be working in an organized and efficient environment that feels good and that motivates you. You will be more productive if you headquarter your campaign from a home office or some location other than your kitchen table. You'll want to direct your campaign and take action from a place that empowers you to work hard and intelligently, one that provides access to a computer, printer, the Internet, a fax machine, and a filing system. You'll need privacy to think and to focus on your daily tasks and objectives.

Perhaps you can create a home office. Or possibly you'll use the public library as your campaign headquarters. The point is that your job campaign office must be similar to a political campaign headquarters—functional, motivating, and highly productive. If you enjoy going to a productive and comfortable campaign headquarters every day, your campaign will have a much better chance to land the job you want sooner than you think. If this represents a challenge for you, become creative and resourceful, because you must work in an environment that inspires you. It is best to work from a campaign headquarters that has no distractions, where you are not interrupted and can concentrate and take action to land a job quickly.

Take Action and Dress to Win

In the same way that an inspiring headquarters enhances and advances your job campaign, how you dress determines how you feel, how productive you are, and how quickly you achieve your goals. Waking up in the morning and working on getting a job while you are wearing your pajamas isn't the dress code that will put you in a peak-performing state of mind. You wouldn't show up to work for an employer in your underwear, and you shouldn't show up working on your next job dressed like that either. During the day, you want to dress as if you will meet your next employer at any time. Look and feel professional. Of course, if you're going to spend time at night on the Internet working from home, you can dress down. Keep in mind that what you wear determines how you feel and that how you feel determines the level of success you will achieve. When you work on your job campaign, dress to win!

Take Action and Implement Your Meticulous Action Plan

It's been said that most people know what to do but their lack of success is a result of not doing what they know. I hope by now you have a detailed action plan, your MAP, with a structured weekly schedule of tasks and goals. Now you simply need to hold yourself accountable every day and implement your plan! It's easy to get distracted and procrastinate. Avoid these enemies to success and execute your plan completely. In fact, every day, go the extra mile and do more than what you have down on your MAP because this is the best investment you can make in landing a job quickly. At a time where most of your competition will do the bare minimum, make sure you always demand more of yourself. Take action to implement your MAP. Massive action leads to massive results!

Take Action to Eliminate Obstacles to Success

It is important that you remain laser-focused on your campaign; you want no distractions. If you are experiencing financial challenges, take action and seek out a financial advisor, your accountant, family members, or friends who can help you address and overcome this obstacle. If you have health issues, take action and get medical advice from appropriate sources to best resolve or work through your issues. If you've lost your health insurance, seek advice from a trusted insurance professional or visit a medical center or your doctor and ask for suggestions. *Every problem has a solution if you are committed to finding one.* If you have personal problems that are consuming your thoughts and time, take action and seek counseling, vent to a friend, or find the proper resources to assist you with your concerns. The point of the matter is that you need to invest 100 percent of your resources and energy in implementing your action plan to land a job quickly. So take the necessary action to avoid any distractions that will impair your campaign. No one makes it alone. Success achievement requires putting together a strong and competent team. Identify your obstacles and then recruit the right team members to neutralize and overcome any potential barriers to success.

Take Action to Access Technology

It comes as no surprise that the Internet provides critical information in a timely manner, and access to the Internet is necessary to rapid employment. In fact, some companies and organizations won't accept résumés unless submitted electronically. It's also important to be skilled in the use of the latest technologies and software. Cover letters need to be personalized, résumés need to be tweaked to align with differing job requirements, and short but personalized thank you e-mails or letters must be sent out after each interview and network meeting.

Access to the Internet is important because company websites provide information that will better prepare you for interviews. We have covered the importance of social media in creating professional LinkedIn and Facebook profiles and using LinkedIn to research companies and people you may want to connect with to get your foot in the door. Most libraries provide computer services and Internet access if you don't have your own. Perhaps you can make arrangements to use the computer of a family member or friend, so long as you have privacy and the ability to focus on the tasks at hand. Take action to gain access to the technology you'll need to land a job in today's technology-driven society and job market. Take action and learn a few simple applications, such as Internet research, LinkedIn, Facebook, Outlook, Word, and other online and computer tools so you can optimize your efforts and get the most out of today's technology.

Take Action to Develop Your Personal Sales Force

We covered this in Step 4: networking is the #1 way to land a job quickly. No other strategy comes close. In a competitive market a good majority of job openings are filled with people who know the hiring manager or who are in the hiring manager's sphere of influence. In other words, a good percentage of jobs are never advertised, or they are filled before they're posted or advertised. This way of acquiring jobs has been, over the years, referred to as the *hidden job market*, even though it is not hidden at all. The term simply means that job openings are filled through the networking process, where people know people or refer people to employers to fill open positions. Taking action toward networking and creating new contacts are activities that are more important today than ever before.

Networking can be enjoyable because you're actually developing your own personal sales force! Remember, you are not asking people you know for a job. Rather, you are asking them to tap into their network of people to access someone they know who can assist you in landing a job. Max Messmer, chairman and CEO of Robert Half International, Inc., one of the world's largest specialized staffing firms, says that "the biggest mistake most job seekers make when it comes to networking is not doing enough of it. The vast majority of jobs—as many as 80 percent by most estimates—are filled today by people who first heard about a job opportunity informally, through another person. So no matter how many people you have in your network, it's never enough."

Just about everybody knows at least 200 people: family, friends, the dry cleaner, the dentist, neighbors, and so on. If your 200 people each know another 200 people, you have a potential network, or sales force, of 40,000 people! And even if everybody you know just knows 100 people each, this represents a network, or sales force, of 10,000 people. Messmer also suggests that "you must add new contacts to your network every week; 10 new contacts a week is not an unreasonable goal." If 10 new people know 200 people, that's an additional 2,000 potential contacts added to your network every week!

Tim Best, principal and senior vice president of client services for Bradley-Morris, Inc., one of the nation's largest military job placement recruiters, says:

> Get LinkedIn! Build a professional and complete profile with the same care and concern you would build your résumé. Then utilize this wonderful networking tool to introduce yourself to actual decision-makers. In most cases you can randomly connect with and contact anyone on LinkedIn. But if you cannot, you can request introductions through people you know. This is an excellent and highly effective way to get "referred" to someone in a hiring mode. Also, network with association leaders. Almost every industry has an association, or multiple associations, that assists in matching qualified association members seeking work with industry employers. This is becoming a primary member benefit and you'll be pleasantly surprised how

cooperative most association leaders are in providing information to help you secure a new job!

When you speak with a networking contact by phone or in person, you want to be sure you end the conversation achieving one or more of the following objectives:

1. Get advice and information that will help you conduct a more efficient, effective, and focused campaign.
2. Get an introduction to someone who knows of an existing job opening.
3. Get the name of a recruiter, a company, or an organization that might be seeking a person with your skills and qualifications.
4. Get referrals to people who may know other people who can help you identify and secure employment opportunities.
5. Get a follow-up meeting or phone conversation with your contacts who might be able to provide additional leads or information after checking in with their own contacts.

When you speak with people from your network, be specific about what you want from them. Don't waste their time or put them in an uncomfortable position. "Help, I'm looking for any kind of job" won't work in most cases. "I am seeking your advice and information on how best to secure an entry-level accounting position, and any help you might be able to provide would be greatly appreciated" is a much more effective and professional approach. Be respectful of their time and precise in communicating what kind of help you are seeking.

Caution: Do not back your contacts into a corner by asking for a job. By doing so, you place them in an uncomfortable and awkward position, and as a result, they will most likely avoid you from that point on. The networking process is one where you are seeking advice and information. If an opportunity is presented to you by your contact, then of course, pursue it. Offer to provide a résumé, and following your discussions with your contacts, always send or e-mail a thank you note.

You can't avoid networking. In a global job market where millions of people are seeking jobs, the people you know and the contacts you establish are critical to rapid employment.

Take Action to Ace the Interview

You can't afford not to close the deal and get a job offer once you get to the interview process; you've come too far. You worked hard to stay positive throughout the job campaign. You defined your goal, created your résumé, and produced powerful communication tools. You developed a well-designed MAP and implemented your action plan with painstaking precision. Now comes the moment of truth. After all the positive and enthusiastic energy invested in your job campaign, it all comes down to the interview. And you must be as well prepared for the interview as presidential candidates are for their televised debates! The problem is that most job seekers are not well prepared to interview, do not use video and camcorder technology when they practice, and do not prepare for the unexpected. The good news for you is that if you do prepare well, you'll do well in the interview.

The interview is an equal encounter between two parties—one who has a position to fill and one who wishes to fill that position. Unquestionably, one of the greatest human fears is that of public speaking. This might help explain why so many people have a fear of interviews. An interview is nothing more than a public speaking engagement in a private setting. In fact, it's more challenging because interviewees (job seekers) have not been given their scripts for the interview. They don't always know what will be asked or what to expect. In addition to the fear of public speaking, another significant reason most people are uncomfortable in an interview is that they feel they are being judged. They don't view an interview as a two-way, equal conversation. They feel totally vulnerable.

Then, there are those job candidates who believe they interview well. These are people who feel comfortable interviewing and are able to build good rapport and communicate well. Yet the truth is, in most cases, they do not differentiate themselves from other qualified candidates. They do not communicate what value-added benefits they bring to the job that makes them better qualified than their competition. The general consensus among the majority of hiring professionals is that most job seekers are not prepared enough for interviews, undersell themselves, and fail to make a clear case for why they are the best candidates for the job.

The Interview Is a Meeting

The employment interview is just a meeting. Although you shouldn't, by any means, treat this meeting lightly, you must keep in mind that there is a mutual need. You need a job, and the company or organization needs an employee. In fact, it's possible the organization interviewing you may need you more than you need a job! So the key to acing the interview is to be well prepared. There are two important aspects to being well prepared: (1) you need to be prepared to convince the interviewer that you can do the job as well as or better than other candidates, and (2) you need to be prepared to convince the interviewer that you're a good fit for the organization.

You Can Do the Job as Well as or Better Than Other Candidates

One of the habits that Dr. Stephen Covey discussed in his book 7 *Habits of Highly Effective People* is, "Seek first to understand, then to be understood." I'm not sure preparing for an interview can be summed up any better. You must know what the company's needs are. You need to know what the organization's problems are. You must know why a position is open. You must know what the company's goals and objectives are. And then you need to blow your own horn confidently, not arrogantly, and convince interviewers that you understand all this. You must persuade them that your presence at the interview is primarily to demonstrate, beyond any doubt, that you can meet their needs, solve their problems, and help them achieve their goals.

Hiring professionals want to know if you have done your homework and are knowledgeable about their company's products, services, history, reputation, personnel, mission statement, and values. Yes, it's a one-way courtship at first. But once a company or an organization sees how much you know about it, it will want to know all about you. So, know the company, know the job you are interviewing for, know the industry the company is in, and know your most valuable skills qualifications and abilities that will convince a prospective employer that you are the best candidate for the job. And, of course, know the results you can produce and contributions you can make.

You're a Good Fit

Once you have proved that you are qualified and have the skills and qualifications to do the job, the final piece to the interviewing puzzle is demonstrating to the interviewer that you are a good fit for the company or organization. People hire people they feel comfortable with and those who share common values. Said differently, *people hire people they like.* You must arrive at the interview knowing the company's values and culture. In most cases, this information is easily accessible on the company's website. If, for instance, you know that a company's values include honesty and integrity and going the extra mile to provide groundbreaking levels of customer service, you must communicate that you share these traits during the interview. If a friend works for the company you are interviewing with and informs you that the company expects its employees to work late hours and occasional weekends, if you want a job offer, you must let the interviewer know during the interview that you are willing to work long hours, including weekends. Other characteristics that might make up a company's culture include dress code, personality, pace, social interaction, and industry commitment.

Behavioral-Based Questions

Most interviewers conduct what are often referred to as behavioral-based interviews. Actually, "case study" or "situational" interviews would better describe this type of interview. A behavioral-based interview is made up of open-ended questions that ask you to illustrate and explain actual circumstances (or situations) that you have previously faced. The interviewers want you to detail specific events, projects, or situations you've encountered in the past and the skills and intellect you used to address them. And, of course, they want to know the results you produced and contributions you made. Behavioral-based interviews predict future performance based on past performance. For candidates new to the job market, such as college graduates or first-time workers, behavioral-based questions may be hypothetical and "what-if " inquiries such as, "If this were to occur while on the job, how would you react?" or "If you experienced a problem working with a peer, what steps would you take to resolve the problem?"

In truth, behavioral-based interviews are more interactive and pro-vide you with more control of the interview than you might realize. You have greater control because you can both answer the question and provide additional information that you feel might be valuable to differentiate you from your competition. Haven't you watched presi-dential debates where candidates are asked questions that they answer quickly (or not at all) and then move on to a completely different and unrelated subject? They do this intentionally because they want to take control of the debate (interview) by addressing what they feel the audi-ence wants and needs to hear. This is how they get elected. And this is how you get hired! You must address the subjects and issues that you know—based on your research—interviewers want to hear that will inevitably tip the hiring scale in your favor.

Behavioral-based interviews are an ideal forum to seal the deal! Be fully prepared. Come into the interview knowing your value and how you can benefit the company. And come prepared with stories, examples, and case studies to offer evidence that you are well qualified for the job. Be honest, confident, and authentic. Go into the interview expecting to enjoy an informative two-way discussion. Let me share with you five important tips so you can enjoy the process and interview effectively to land the job you came to interview for:

1. *Be prepared for tough questions.* Anticipate those questions that are uncomfortable for you. Then script out answers so you become totally comfortable with them. Don't be caught off guard!

2. *Don't let unlawful questions rattle you.* Ellen Block, my wife and an employment law attorney, says:

> Unlawful interview questions are questions that are not directly job-related which attempt to elicit information about race, color, ances-try, age, gender, religion, and/or disability, unless based upon bona fide occupational qualifications. If you are asked such a question, you should professionally and tactfully ask the interviewer about the business-basis for the question before you answer. For example, if asked your age, you could respond by saying, "I'm happy to answer your question, but can you clarify for me the business reason for your

question?" or if you are asked "What church do you attend?" you may reply by saying, "In preparation for my interview today, I thoroughly reviewed the qualifications and I admit I was not prepared to answer that question, as church attendance was not listed as a qualification. But if this position requires it, I will be happy to answer." Understandably, this is not easy or comfortable to articulate for many people, but your honesty and respectful straightforwardness may just gain you points in the interview. However, if an unlawful question is asked for a seemingly well-intentioned reason and it does not offend you or cause a hiring concern, stay calm and just answer it in an effective and confident way. The goal is to win the job offer. Then, based on how you feel after you've been offered the job, you determine if you'll accept it or not.

3. *Be prepared to ask good questions.* Hiring professionals are placing more and more weight on the quality of the questions you ask them in interviews. Prepare four or five intelligent, provocative, and sensible questions that will indicate you take the interview as seriously as they do.

4. *Be ready to handle the subject of salary.* If the subject of salary comes up during the interview, the general rule is to try and avoid it until an offer has been made. This is because the greatest leverage you have is after the job offer but before acceptance. However, you may have no choice but to discuss salary when asked about your salary requirements or salary history. You must know, in advance, the salary range for the job you are seeking and then provide a realistic range; "I would expect the job to pay between $30,000 and $40,000, and I believe, based on my value to your company, we can agree to an amicable number." Or "Over the past five years, my salary has been between $80,000 and $93,000. I plan to make a significant contribution to your sales efforts, so my starting salary is less important than the ability to demonstrate to you that I can produce results. And I am sure when you see the results I can produce, my salary will reflect those contributions." Once again, I emphasize that if you know your value and how you can contribute and benefit the organization, you'll feel in control when negotiating a win-win compensation arrangement.

5. *Follow up*. First and without exception, always mail and/or e-mail a thank you note within hours following an interview. Unless you have a reason to do otherwise, keep the message short and subtly show your interest to move forward in the hiring process. "Thank you for taking the time to meet with me this afternoon. I am confident that I am highly qualified for this job and look forward to the next step in the hiring process." After the interview, maintain professional contact with the interviewer. If the interviewer tells you that you'll be contacted in a week, wait the full week. If you don't hear back in a week, a phone call or e-mail is appropriate. Stay in touch with the interviewer, but also be keenly aware of that fine line between staying in touch and being a nuisance—and don't cross it.

Background Checks

Andrew J. Tabone, former recruitment manager for Carnival Cruise Lines, says:

> Preemployment criminal background, credit, and drug tests are requisite conditions for most full-time positions as well as for temporary contract engagement work. This is no longer reserved for larger employers these days. Candidates may successfully make it through the rigors of applying for, interviewing for, and receiving a job offer, only to be undone by what they thought was a minor dispute years ago that unexpectedly turns up on a police report. And candidates fail drug tests more often than one might expect. So I suggest that job candidates ensure that their "background" is positioned so that it does not sabotage their job campaign goals. If you think a company won't check on something that might be problematic for you, I suggest you think again. Do all you can do, including mending fences with former employers who might provide poor references, and alleviate problems that stand in the way of a permanent job offer.

One way to manage your background and references is to Google your name and know what employers will see when they research your background. Today, many employers conduct a myriad of background checks or hire companies to perform the search. So it is important to know what they will find so you can best address and resolve potential problems. Employers are conducting background checks that include driving records, vehicle registrations, credit records, bankruptcy records, criminal records, education records, court records, workers' compensation claims, medical records, property ownership, military records, drug test records, past employers, and personal references. Be prepared and seek out assistance from authoritative sources if there are areas that you need to address in an interview but are unsure how best to do so.

An Employment Proposal

Finally, let me introduce you to the concept of an employment proposal, yet another unique strategy for getting a job through a familiar, everyday sales and marketing practice. A universally accepted and expected sales approach is for sales professionals to present their products and services to prospective buyers and to provide a proposal (or a price) for those products and services. If you are purchasing a home or automobile, for example, the sellers provide a proposal, or price, from which you can begin negotiations. In most cases, sellers provide proposals or prices to prospective buyers to initiate a successful seller-buyer transaction.

When selling yourself in a competitive job market, you are the sales professional. Prospective buyers, aka employers, are meeting with you to determine if you are the right candidate for the job. This sales meeting, otherwise known as an interview, takes place. So here's a question to ponder. If you are the sales professional (job seeker) and are selling yourself and your skills to a would-be buyer (potential employer), why would you wait for the buyer to make a proposal? In most other sales encounters, the seller makes the proposal! An employment proposal is a proactive, formal, written document submitted to a prospective employer offering your services and outlining a proposed employment arrangement. In the same way a business consultant would submit a proposal to a company for consulting services, you submit a proposal to a prospective employer for employment services.

If the interview went well and there are no apparent snags to getting to the next step of the hiring process or to getting a potential job offer, an employment proposal would NOT be recommended. The employment proposal can be highly effective when:

- You feel you might not be the strongest candidate for the job
- You were not offered the job or were rejected but still "have a chance"
- The hiring process has been delayed for an unknown reason
- You want to propose that a company create a new job that does not currently exist but that would benefit the company
- You want to be considered as an independent contractor as opposed to an employee
- You want to stand out and can afford to be professionally aggressive

Make Them an Offer They Can't Refuse

The employment proposal is an innovative and effective method for demonstrating initiative. Drive and initiative are viewed favorably by many employers. They show that you are an enterprising individual. In today's job market, you must view yourself as self-employed and use every effective marketing tool to promote yourself to potential employers. An employment proposal is similar to any other proposal. It is an effective promotional instrument that communicates the distinct advantages you offer and the results you can deliver. Here is a sample employment proposal.

MELINDA GRANT

1234 8th Street • Freemont, MI 40002

(505) 555–6722 • e-mail@e-mail.com

March 14, 20xx

Mr. James Allen, President

S.D. Allen & Company

9955 33rd Place

Freemont, MI 44403

Dear Mr. Allen:

Thank you for meeting with me yesterday. I thoroughly enjoyed meeting with you and your staff, touring your plant, and discussing the position of Accounts Receivable Manager. I am confident I can reduce your average outstanding accounts receivable from your present level of 68 days down to 32–35 days without compromising customer relations. As we discussed, this would free up over $200k in cash.

My Proposal

There is no doubt in my mind that I can produce the results you want and work collaboratively with your staff. Furthermore, we share common values including professionalism, a strong work ethic, and providing extraordinary customer service in a team-spirited way. These values along with the value of "accountability" make me a good fit for your company.

I propose to you that I work for your company for a probationary period of 120 days. In that time, you can expect me to:

- Develop a credit policy that will improve customer relations and reduce A/R.
- Slash the average A/R aging from 68 days to 45 days in 120 days, with the goal of achieving 32–35 days within 6–9 months.
- Demonstrate that I have the skills and personality to warrant continued employment.

If, after 120 days, I have not met the goals or fit in with your culture, I will voluntarily resign, I will not file an unemployment claim, and we part amicably. But I do not expect that to happen. You will see that I will be a valuable asset to your accounting department.

I would be willing to work at the lower end of the salary range that we discussed, secure in knowing that my performance will dictate future earnings. And I would be able to begin working on Monday, the 27th.

I hope you will give this proposal serious consideration, and I look forward to discussing this with you.

Sincerely,

Melinda Grant

Note: For more detailed information on winning interview strategies, please refer to my book *Great Answers! Great Questions! for Your Job Interview*, which I coauthored with Michael Betrus.

STEP 5 SUMMARY

- Knowledge is not power. Knowledge is potential power. Power and success come from taking action on what you know. The fifth and final step of the five-step job campaign process is taking action.
- Take action and establish your campaign headquarters. Don't minimize the importance of having an inspiring place from which to conduct your job campaign.
- Take action and dress to win. The way you dress also determines the way you feel, your productivity, and your outcome.
- Take action to eliminate obstacles to success. You must devote 100 percent of your resources and energy toward implementing your action plan to land the job you want at the pay you deserve.
- Take action to access technology. The Internet provides critical information in a timely manner that is necessary to land a job in any job market.
- Take massive action and network to build your personal sales force. A good percentage of jobs are never advertised, or they are filled before they're advertised. More than ever, it's who you know and who you meet that will result in your next job, not what you know or how good you are.
- Keep adding people to your network. Get LinkedIn and use Facebook and other social networking sites, as long as your presence is strictly professional, to network and expand your network. When it comes to making new contacts and building new relationships, you can never have enough.
- Do not ask people in your network for a job. The networking process is one where you seek advice and information, not a job. You are looking for job leads or names of other people who might help you.
- The interview is an equal encounter between two parties—one who has a position to fill and one who wishes to fill that position. Treat the interview as just a meeting, and be as well prepared for the interview as presidential candidates are for their televised

debates! Convince the interviewer that you can do the job as well as or better than other candidates.

- Prepare to convince the interviewer that you're a good fit for the company. You need to communicate confidently that you understand the company's needs, problems, and goals and can be an asset in successfully addressing them. Companies and organizations hire people they like.

- Be prepared to answer behavioral-based, or "case study" or "situational," questions. A behavioral-based interview is made up of open-ended questions that ask you to illustrate and explain actual circumstances that you have previously faced. Behavioral-based questions for candidates new to the job market, such as college graduates or first-time workers, may be hypothetical and "what-if" inquiries such as, "If this were to occur while on the job, how would you react?"

- If the subject of salary comes up during the interview, the general rule is to try and avoid it until an offer has been made. This is because the greatest leverage you have is after the job offer but before acceptance. But you must be prepared to confidently discuss salary at any time the subject comes up when it can't be avoided.

- Always mail or e-mail a thank you note within hours following an interview. Unless you have a reason to do otherwise, keep the message short and subtly show your interest to move forward in the hiring process.

- Be sure your references and "background" are in order so they don't sabotage a job offer. If potential problems exist, address and resolve them so your campaign is not unnecessarily prolonged.

- Under the right circumstance, consider using an employment proposal. An employment proposal is a proactive, formal, written document submitted to a prospective employer offering your services and outlining a proposed employment arrangement.

AUTHOR'S FINAL COMMENT

When I was fired by one of my best friends back in 1992, there were five concepts my coaches taught me that made the most difference in helping me deal with, and overcome, my pain and disappointment. These concepts helped me identify a meaningful and exciting career when, at the time, I hadn't a clue what I wanted to do for a living at age 39. I would go so far as to say that these five ideas changed and actually saved my life. So let me conclude by sharing with you these five concepts, knowing that if you embrace these messages, they will serve you as well as they have served me.

1. *I learned that it's not the wind that blows that really matters; rather, it's the set of the sail that makes all the difference.* I was taught that some things are out of my control. I can't control getting a lousy boss or getting fired, much like I can't control the way the wind blows. But what I can control is how I set the sail, how I respond and react to the wind. When I realized that I alone control how I think and feel, no matter what the situation, I was able to achieve whatever I set my mind on achieving. The same holds true for you!

2. *I learned not to wish that things were easier; rather, that I was better.* I discovered that life is not about easy; it's about purpose, meaning, passion, love, contribution, sacrifice, and hard work. I discovered that life is about creating all that I can create in the short time that I'm on this planet. So I stopped wishing to find the shortcuts and employed discipline and hard work to make my dreams comes true. The same holds true for you!

3. *I learned that I am what I think; I am my thoughts.* I was taught to be the master of my own thoughts, because if I think I can do something, I will. And if I doubt I can do something, I won't. I learned that

my thoughts are the blueprints for my future. So I changed my beliefs and I challenged myself to rethink what I thought I knew. And when I developed new empowering thoughts and beliefs, everything changed for me. The same is true for you!

4. *I learned that if I didn't plant in the spring, I'd have to beg in the fall.* I learned that with everything in life, including my career, I had to plant the seeds of achievement so I could reap the rewards. I learned that I had to plant seeds of new ideas, new beliefs, and new commitments every day in order to find happiness and meaning in a new career and in my life. The same philosophy is true for you!

5. *Finally, I learned that I had to enjoy the journey in pursuit of the destination.* I have to admit, to this day, this remains one of my toughest challenges. But my teachers taught me that I have to be happy with what I have in pursuit of what I want. And yes, I discovered that true joy comes from living in the moment, enjoying the journey to the top. I discovered that every moment is a precious gift, because future moments are, in no way, guaranteed. The same is true for you!

And finally, beware of doubt. Never doubt yourself, who you are or the goals you are capable of achieving. Shakespeare said, "Our doubts are traitors and make us lose the good we oft might win, by fearing to attempt."

I wish you success in all future endeavors!

ACKNOWLEDGMENTS

I owe a debt of gratitude to hundreds of people from around the globe over the past 20 years who have helped shape me as an industry professional. It would take dozens of pages to name all of them, and I'm sure I would omit many key names from that list. So to all those with whom I have had the pleasure and honor of sharing experiences over the years, thank you for your friendships, contributions, and support.

This is my twelfth book published by McGraw-Hill, and I am grateful that the publisher has given me the opportunity to produce works that help affect people's lives in a positive way. This book is the most important one I have ever written, and a book that is sorely needed in a complex, competitive global job market. *Five Steps to Rapid Employment* is the only motivational career book of its kind that is also process oriented. Indeed, most of us can use as much motivation as we can get and a process for rapid employment that actually works.

I want to especially thank my editor, Dannalie Diaz, because this book would not have been published without her unwavering and enthusiastic support. I also want to thank my editorial director, Mary Glenn, for her continued support over all the years I have been with McGraw-Hill. And a special thank you to Janice Race, senior editing supervisor, who always makes the editing process enjoyable and the deadlines reasonable. I also want to extend a warm thank you to my copyeditor, Judy Duguid. Once again, she treated this manuscript as though it were her own and provided clear evidence that I should have paid more attention in my English classes back in grade and high school.

My particular thanks go to Frank Fox, executive director of the Professional Association of Résumé Writers and Career Coaches, and to Dick Bolles, author of *What Color Is Your Parachute?* for his support and for opening the industry doors for many of us some 40 years ago. I also want to thank Bob Burg, author of *Endless Referrals* and *The Go-Giver*; Rob Thomson, managing partner of Waterfront Properties & Club Communities in Jupiter, Florida; Tim Best, principal and senior vice president for Bradley-Morris, Inc., a national career placement firm for veterans; Andrew J. Tabone, former recruitment and career development manager at Carnival Cruise Lines; Sherry Zylka, PhD, provost, Wayne County Community College District, Michigan; Martin Buckland, master career coach in Ontario, Canada; Susan J. Cook, former executive vice president and chief human resources officer for Eaton Corporation; Susan Leventhal, PPN manager, Workforce One, South Florida; and Susan D. Corey of the Southeast Michigan Community Alliance, manager of Workforce Development, and board member of the National Association of Workforce Development Professionals for writing the foreword to the book.

I want to thank my sister-in-law, Ina-Lee Block, for her help with the cover of the book. And, finally, I want to thank my wife, Ellen, for supporting me in every way and in every aspect of writing this book.

INDEX

ABOUT THE AUTHOR

Jay Block is an industry pioneer and one of the nation's leading motivational career and empowerment coaches. He is the author of 18 career and motivational books, 12 of which are published by McGraw-Hill. Jay is a highly respected trainer and keynote presenter and is best known for combining  world-class motivational techniques with cutting-edge job campaign tools and strategies that result in rapid success. He works with job seekers who are unemployed, underemployed, unhappily employed, and happily employed wanting to advance. Jay created seven international certification programs for career coaches and trainers, including his award-winning program, Five Steps to Rapid Employment™. He travels the country to share his ideas and concepts with job seekers and employment professionals. Jay lives in South Florida and can be reached by visiting his website at www.jayblock.com.